WORKB

Focus on Grammar

A **BASIC** Course for Reference and Practice

SECOND EDITION

Samuela Eckstut

Focus on Grammar: A **Basic** Course for Reference and Practice
Workbook

Copyright © 2000, 1994 by Addison Wesley Longman, Inc.
A Pearson Education Company.

Pearson Education, 10 Bank Street, White Plains, NY 10606

Editorial director: Allen Ascher
Executive editor: Louisa Hellegers
Director of design and production: Rhea Banker
Development editor: Lise Minovitz
Production manager: Alana Zdinak
Managing editor: Linda Moser
Senior production editor: Virginia Bernard
Production editor: Christine Lauricella
Senior manufacturing manager: Patrice Fraccio
Manufacturing supervisor: David Dickey
Cover design: Rhea Banker
Text design adaptation: Rainbow Graphics
Text composition: Rainbow Graphics
Illustrator: Dave Sullivan

ISBN: 0–201–34685–0

3 4 5 6 7 8 9 10—BAH—04 03 02 01

Contents

ABOUT THE AUTHOR

Samuela Eckstut has taught ESL and EFL for twenty years, in the United States, Greece, Italy, and England. Currently she is teaching at Boston University, Center for English Language and Orientation Programs (CELOP). She has authored or co-authored numerous texts for the teaching of English, notably *What's in a Word? Reading and Vocabulary Building; In the Real World; First Impressions; Beneath the Surface; Widely Read;* and *Finishing Touches.*

UNIT

PRESENT AND PRESENT PROGRESSIVE; HOW OFTEN . . . ?; ADVERBS AND EXPRESSIONS OF FREQUENCY

① THE SIMPLE PRESENT TENSE AND ADVERBS OF FREQUENCY

Put a check (✓) next to the sentences that are true.

_____ 1. Americans almost always have dinner after nine o'clock.

_____ 2. Americans never celebrate birthdays.

_____ 3. Americans often give a present on a friend's or relative's birthday.

_____ 4. Americans rarely ski to work.

_____ 5. Americans always eat rice with dinner.

_____ 6. There are seldom fireworks on July 4th in the United States.

_____ 7. Americans don't usually drink tea at five o'clock in the afternoon.

_____ 8. Thanksgiving is always on a Thursday.

_____ 9. Americans sometimes work on Sundays.

_____ 10. Americans don't often drink coffee in the morning.

② THE SIMPLE PRESENT TENSE AND ADVERBS OF FREQUENCY

Underline the correct adverbs or expressions of frequency. Then write sentences.

1. The doctor says, "I go to the hospital."

   (rarely, <u>usually</u>) __I usually go to the hospital.__

2. The police officer says, "I arrest people."

   (<u>sometimes</u>, never) __I sometimes arrest people.__

(continued on next page)

3. The football player says, "I practice in the middle of the night."

   (always, rarely) _____

4. The salesperson says, "I fight with customers."

   (always, seldom) _____

5. The taxi driver says, "I drive at night."

   (never, often) _____

6. The pharmacist says, "I'm careful."

   (always, rarely) _____

7. The mechanic says, "I find the problem with the car."

   (almost always, seldom) _____

8. The chef says, "I put lemon in milk."

   (never, often) _____

9. The factory worker says, "I'm bored."

   (never, once in a while) _____

10. The nurse says, "The hospital is open."

    (every day, frequently) _____

11. The firefighter says, "I wear a suit and tie to work."

    (every day, almost never) _____

12. The flight attendant says, "We're away from home for three or four days."

    (frequently, never) _____

❸ QUESTIONS WITH *HOW OFTEN*

Write questions. Use **how often**. *Then answer the questions. Use the information in the chart.*

	SWIM	PLAY BASKETBALL	DO EXERCISES	JOG
BARBARA	three times a week	never	every day	rarely
DONNA	once in a while	frequently	four times a week	five days a week
DAVID	never	almost every day	every morning	rarely
ED	once or twice a week	never	never	often
GEORGE	once or twice a week	almost every day	almost every day	almost never

1. (Barbara / do exercises)

    How often does Barbara do exercises?

    She does exercises every day.

2. (Donna / play basketball)

    _____

    _____

3. (David / swim)

    _____

    _____

4. (Barbara and Ed / play basketball)

    _____

    _____

(continued on next page)

5. (Ed / jog)

_____

_____

6. (Barbara / swim)

_____

_____

7. (Barbara and David / jog)

_____

_____

8. (Ed and George / swim)

_____

_____

9. (George and David / play basketball)

_____

_____

10. (George / jog)

_____

_____

11. (you / jog)

_____

_____

12. (you / do exercises)

_____

_____

4 THE SIMPLE PRESENT TENSE

Match the occupations with the activities.

1. __i__ artists
2. ____ bakers
3. ____ bank tellers
4. ____ bus drivers
5. ____ butchers
6. ____ doctors
7. ____ gardeners
8. ____ mechanics
9. ____ newspaper reporters
10. ____ scientists
11. ____ waitresses
12. ____ zookeepers

a. bake bread and cake
b. count money
c. cut meat
d. do experiments
e. drive buses
f. examine patients
g. feed animals
h. fix cars
i. paint pictures
j. serve food
k. water plants and flowers
l. write articles

5 THE SIMPLE PRESENT TENSE VS. THE PRESENT PROGRESSIVE

Complete the sentences. Use the correct form of the verbs in Exercise 4.

1. Scott's a doctor. He _____examines patients_____ every day. Right now he's in his office. He _____is ('s) examining a patient_____.

2. Marilyn's a bus driver. She _____ five days a week. Right now she's at work. She _____.

3. Larry's a mechanic. Every day he _____. Right now he's at his garage. He _____.

4. Anne's a waitress. Every day she _____. Right now she's at the restaurant. She _____.

5. Sandra and Pat are artists. They _____ almost every day. Right now they're both at their studios. They _____.

6. Nicholas and Catherine are scientists. They _____ every day. Right now they're in the lab. They _____.

7. Renée and Cathy are newspaper reporters. They _____ every afternoon. They're at work right now. They _____.

(continued on next page)

8. Arthur's a butcher. He _____ every day. Right now he's at his store. He _____.

9. Linda's a bank teller. She _____ all day long. Right now she's at the bank. She _____.

10. Barry and Fred are bakers. They _____ every morning. They're in the kitchen now. They _____.

11. Ruth's a gardener. She _____ almost every day. Right now she's at work. She _____.

12. Jeffrey's a zookeeper. He _____ two times a day. Right now he's in the elephant house. He _____.

---

6 **THE SIMPLE PRESENT TENSE VS. THE PRESENT PROGRESSIVE**

Complete the telephone conversation. Use the correct form of the verbs in parentheses.

MARSHA: Hello.

ALAN: Hi, Marsha. This is Alan.

MARSHA: Oh, hi, Alan.

ALAN: What _____ are you doing _____ right now?
              1. (you / do)
_____ anything important?
       2. (you / do)

MARSHA: No, I _____ some vegetables for dinner. That's all.
                3. (cut)

ALAN: _____ dinner at this time every evening?
       4. (you / prepare)

MARSHA: Yeah, usually. We _____ at around 8:00. Why? When
                    5. (eat)
_____ dinner?
    6. (you / have)

ALAN: Oh, my family and I _____ much earlier, probably
                    7. (eat)
because our kids _____ to bed by 7:30. In fact, they
              8. (go)
_____ ready for bed right now.
    9. (get)

MARSHA: Really? Our daughter _____ to bed until 9:30,
10. (not go)

sometimes even ten o'clock. _____ to bed so early on
11. (your kids / go)

the weekends, too?

ALAN: No, but they _____ later than 8:30. They
12. (not stay up)

_____ at around 6:30 every morning, so they
13. (get up)

_____ tired by then. What
14. (be)

_____ all evening? _____ a
15. (your daughter / do)   16. (she / watch)

lot of television?

MARSHA: No, she _____ the violin. Actually, she
17. (practice)

_____ right now.
18. (practice)

ALAN: How often _____?
19. (she / practice)

MARSHA: Every day for at least an hour.

ALAN: You're kidding. _____ well?
20. (she / play)

MARSHA: Very well. We _____ very proud of her.
21. (be)

ALAN: I'm sure. Listen, I _____ on a report for the office, and
22. (work)

there _____ a problem.
23. (be)

_____ a couple of minutes to talk to me about it?
24. (you / have)

MARSHA: Sure.

NON-ACTION VERBS

❶ ACTION VERBS VS. NON-ACTION VERBS

Underline the verb in each sentence. Then write **action verb** *or* **non-action verb**.

1. I <u>have</u> a car. _____*non-action verb*_____

2. She <u>drives</u> badly. _____*action verb*_____

3. I don't have any brothers or sisters. _____

4. Mitchell is having lunch. _____

5. This book belongs to me. _____

6. What do you need? _____

7. Do you like horror movies? _____

8. Do they come by bus every day? _____

9. Do the flowers smell nice? _____

10. Why are you smelling the milk? _____

11. We do a lot of grammar exercises
    in this class. _____

12. Why does he hate chocolate? _____

13. I don't know the answer. _____

14. Where are they running? _____

➋ THE SIMPLE PRESENT TENSE VS. THE PRESENT PROGRESSIVE

Complete the sentences. Circle the correct answers and write them on the lines.

1. I _____have_____ ten dollars. The money's in my bag.

   a. have

   b. am having

2. We _____ help. Let's ask the teacher.

   a. need

   b. are needing

3. I'm busy. I _____ on the phone.

   a. talk

   b. am talking

4. She _____ it. Explain it to her again.

   a. does not understand

   b. is not understanding

5. Pedro _____ his family. That's why he's sad.

   a. misses

   b. is missing

6. You _____ in the right place. Look over there!

   a. do not look

   b. are not looking

7. There's a problem, but I _____ the answer.

   a. do not know

   b. am not knowing

8. I _____. Don't talk to me!

   a. think

   b. am thinking

(continued on next page)

9. That shirt _____ good. Buy it!

   a. looks

   b. is looking

10. _____ that guy is nice?

    a. Do you think

    b. Are you thinking

11. There's a car outside. _____ to you?

    a. Does it belong

    b. Is it belonging

12. The little boy is unhappy. That's why he _____.

    a. cries

    b. is crying

13. Let's stay. I _____ a good time.

    a. have

    b. am having

14. That music _____ terrible. Turn it off!

    a. sounds

    b. is sounding

3 **THE SIMPLE PRESENT TENSE VS. THE PRESENT PROGRESSIVE**

Complete the conversation. Write the correct form of the verbs in parentheses. Use contractions if possible.

A: What _____ do you want _____ to do now?
       1. (you / want)

B: I _____. _____ to go to the
       2. (not care)   **3. (you / want)**

    movies?

A: What _____?
       4. (play)

B: I _____. I _____ a newspaper.
       5. (not know)   **6. (not have)**

A: Well, let's go for a walk and get one.

B: But it _____.
          7. (rain)

A: So what? I _____ an umbrella.
                  8. (have)

B: But I _____ one.
           9. (not have)

A: Well, take mine. I _____ it.
                          10. (not need)

I _____ the rain.
   11. (like)

B: Okay.

A: Maybe Alex _____ to come with us.
                  12. (want)

B: I _____ so. He _____ a lot of
        13. (not think)   **14. (have)**

homework tonight. He _____ it right now.
                      15. (do)

A: But I _____ his voice. He _____
            16. (hear)   **17. (talk)**

on the phone.

B: He _____ to a classmate. There's something he
          18. (talk)

_____, and he _____ some help.
19. (not understand)   **20. (get)**

A: How _____?
           21. (you / know)

B: I _____ everything.
        22. (know)

A: Well, you _____ what's playing at the movies. So let's go!
                 23. (not know)

27 VERBS PLUS NOUNS, GERUNDS, AND INFINITIVES

❶ VERBS

Match the sentences with the speakers. (Look at your Student Book if you need help.)

1. __d__ I want to clean the apartment.

2. _____ All of you need to study more.

3. _____ My daughter-in-law does not like to take care of my son.

4. _____ My daughter does not like studying very much.

5. _____ I prefer to wear baggy jeans.

6. _____ I do not enjoy cleaning all the time.

7. _____ I want to speak English perfectly.

8. _____ I'm tired of looking at your pictures.

9. _____ My mother keeps telling me to clean my room.

    a. Pete

    b. Lulu

    c. Doug

    d. Yoko

    e. Carol

    f. Doug

    g. Bertha

    h. Yoko

    i. Norma

❷ GERUNDS

Look at the pictures. Then find the two mistakes in each sentence and correct the mistakes. (Look at the pictures in the Student Book if you need help.)

    Doug   skiing

1. ~~Carol~~ enjoys to ~~ski~~.

2. Pete is good at fix things.

3. Doug enjoys fish.

4. Norma is interested in collect stamps.

5. Lulu enjoys to garden.

6. Yoko is good at to ride horses.

7. Elenore is interested in learn Spanish.

8. Milt is good at cook.

3 VERBS PLUS INFINITIVES AND GERUNDS

Complete the sentences. Write the correct form of the verbs in the box.

be	~~buy~~	help	move	receive
relax	study	swim	study	talk

1. **A:** Why are you going to the store?

   B: I want _____to buy_____ some fruit.

2. **A:** Why do you go to the swimming pool on Sunday mornings?

   B: I prefer _____ on Sundays. It's quiet then.

3. **A:** Why are you angry with your roommate?

   B: She never wants _____ with the housework.

4. **A:** Why are you closing the door?

   B: I need _____ to you in private.

5. **A:** Why are Gina and Louis looking for an apartment?

   B: They want _____ .

6. **A:** Why are they going to the airport so late?

   B: They do not need _____ at the airport until the evening.

7. **A:** Why do you write so many letters?

   B: Because we like _____ them.

8. **A:** Why do you go to the library after class every day?

   B: I prefer _____ there.

9. **A:** Why do you and your wife always stay home on Sundays?

   B: We like _____ .

10. **A:** Why are you putting your books away?

    B: Because I finished _____ .

POSSESSIVE ADJECTIVES AND POSSESSIVE PRONOUNS

❶ POSSESSIVE PRONOUNS

Write **correct** *if the sentence is correct. Write* **car** *in the sentences where a noun is necessary.*

1. Your is not working. _____Your car is not working._____

2. Mine is not working. _____correct_____

3. Is this yours? _____

4. Ours is over there. _____

5. Please bring me my. _____

6. Where is her? _____

7. Give me hers, please. _____

8. Theirs is on Park Street. _____

9. We need our. _____

10. Their is expensive. _____

11. I like mine a lot. _____

12. Why do you want your? _____

❷ POSSESSIVE PRONOUNS

Complete the sentences. Use **mine, yours, his, hers, ours,** *or* **theirs.**

1. That is not her bicycle. _____Hers_____ is blue.

2. That's not my jacket. _____ is gray.

3. **A:** Is that his classroom?

   B: No, _____ is on the fifth floor.

(continued on next page)

4. A: Is that our suitcase?

   B: No, _____ is not light brown. We have a dark brown suitcase.

5. These are not your shoes. _____ are under the bed.

6. A: Is that their house?

   B: No, _____ is on Middle Street.

7. A: Are those your son's sneakers?

   B: No, _____ are a size 12.

8. A: Is that Ms. Gilman's office?

   B: No, _____ is in the next building.

9. These are not Yuri and Natasha's test papers. _____ are on my desk.

10. My roommate and I have a sofa like that one, but _____ is a little bigger.

3 POSSESSIVE ADJECTIVES VS. POSSESSIVE PRONOUNS

Complete the conversations. Use the correct possessive adjective or possessive pronoun.

1. A: This is not _____my_____ coat.

   B: Where's _____yours_____?

   A: In the closet.

2. A: That's _____ ball. Give it to me!

   B: It's not _____. It's _____. It's a birthday present from my brother.

3. A: Whose scarf is this?

   B: It's Nancy's.

   A: Are you sure it's _____? This scarf is green, and she rarely wears green.

   B: I'm sure it's _____.

4. A: We're so happy with _____ new car. We love it.

   B: You're lucky. We don't like _____ at all.

5. A: Do you know Bonnie and Tony Gray? _____ son is on the football team.

   B: We know them, but we don't know _____ son. Our son is on the junior

   high school team, but _____ is on the high school team.

6. A: Is this your husband's hat?

   B: Yes, it is.

   A: How do you know it's _____?

   B: Because all of _____ hats have his name inside.

UNIT

29 REVIEW OF THE SIMPLE PAST TENSE; NEGATIVE QUESTIONS

1 **AFFIRMATIVE AND NEGATIVE STATEMENTS WITH THE SIMPLE PAST TENSE**

Complete the sentences. Use the affirmative or negative form of the verb in parentheses.

1. Yoko ___didn't get___ out of bed
      (get)
at six o'clock yesterday.

2. Then she _____
                    (make)
breakfast.

3. She _____ for class at
          (leave)
half past eight.

4. She and her classmates
_____ all tired.
        (be)

5. She _____ lunch alone.
(have)

6. In the afternoon she _____ golf.
(play)

7. Then she _____ some dog food.
(buy)

8. Then she _____ dinner with Carol.
(eat)

9. After dinner she and Rocky _____ TV.
(watch)

---

2 **YES / NO QUESTIONS AND SHORT ANSWERS WITH THE SIMPLE PAST TENSE**

Answer the questions. Use short answers.

1. Was Carol with her family on Thanksgiving? __No, she wasn't._____

2. Were your parents born in New York? _____

3. Did you buy anything yesterday? _____

4. Was your father a good student? _____

5. Was it cold yesterday? _____

6. Did you take a shower yesterday? _____

7. Were you born in a hospital? _____

(continued on next page)

8. Did your parents get married five years ago? _____

9. Did you and a friend go to the movies last night? _____

10. Was the last grammar exercise easy? _____

11. Did your English teacher give you a test last week? _____

12. Were you absent from your last English class? _____

---

3 **YES / NO QUESTIONS AND SHORT ANSWERS WITH THE PAST TENSE OF *BE***

Write questions and answers. Use the past tense of **be.**

1. **A:** We had a nice holiday.

    B: _Were you with your whole family?_ (you / with your whole family)

    A: _No, my daughter was in Montreal._ (no / my daughter / in Montreal)

2. **A:** I bought these new shoes yesterday.

    B: _____ (they / on sale)

    A: _____ (yes / they / only $25)

3. **A:** _____ (you / at home / last night)

    B: _____ (no / I / at the library)

4. **A:** _____ (the guests / late for the party)

    B: _____ (no / they / all on time)

5. **A:** _____ (it / warm / in Australia)

    B: _____ (the weather / beautiful / every day)

6. **A:** _____ (the movie / good)

    B: _____ (it / okay)

7. **A:** _____ (the people at the party / friendly)

    B: _____ (most of them / very nice)

8. **A:** I called the lawyer.

    B: _____ (he / there)

    A: _____ (no / he / in a meeting)

4 NEGATIVE QUESTIONS

Complete the conversations with negative questions. Use the verbs in parentheses.

1. A: I'm so upset. I think I failed my math test.

    B: _____Didn't you study_____ for it?
                    (study)
    A: Yeah, but it was really difficult.

2. A: I'm really hungry.

    B: _____ breakfast?
                (eat)
    A: No, I didn't have time.

3. A: What's the homework for tomorrow?

    B: _____ in class yesterday?
                (be)
    A: Yeah, but I didn't write down the homework.

4. A: Hi, honey. How's the weather there?

    B: It's raining.

    A: _____ yesterday?
                (rain)
    B: It rains almost everyday here.

5. A: I don't want to go to the Italian restaurant again.

    B: _____ it the last time we went there?
                (like)
    A: Yeah, but we go there so much. I'm tired of the place.

6. A: I was home yesterday morning at nine.

    B: _____ your history class at nine?
                (be)
    A: I didn't go.

7. A: What movie do you want to see?

    B: Why don't we go to *The Lost Island*?

    A: _____ that with Eddie a couple of weeks ago?
                (see)
    B: Yeah, but it was really good. I'd like to see it again.

WH- QUESTIONS IN THE SIMPLE PAST TENSE

1 WH- QUESTIONS IN THE SIMPLE PAST TENSE

Complete the conversations. Circle the correct questions and write them on the lines.

1. **A:** I was absent yesterday.

   B: _What was wrong?_____

      a. Who was absent?   **b.** What was wrong?

   A: I was ill.

2. **A:** We had dinner at the new Mexican restaurant.

   B: _____

      a. How was the food?   **b.** Did you like the food?

   A: Yes. It was very good.

3. **A:** You forgot Cathy's birthday.

   B: _____

      a. When was it?   **b.** Where was she?

   A: Last Thursday.

4. **A:** I went to bed at eight o'clock last night.

   B: _____

      a. What did you do?   **b.** Why were you so tired?

   A: I don't know. I didn't feel very well.

5. **A:** You missed a great party.

   B: _____

      a. Who was there?   **b.** How was the party?

   A: People from our class and their friends.

6. **A:** I found your keys.

B: _____

    a. Where did you find them?   **b.** Why were they there?

A: Under the desk.

7. **A:** I got everything right on the test.

B: _____

    a. Really? Where were the answers to the first and third questions?

    b. Really? What were the answers to the first and third questions?

A: The answer to the first was C, and D was the answer to the third.

8. **A:** We were on vacation for two weeks.

B: _____

    a. Where did you go?   **b.** How was it?

A: It was great.

9. **A:** We had a great time in Hong Kong.

B: _____

    a. Who were you with?   **b.** When did you go there?

A: We were there about two years ago.

10. **A:** I went to a great movie with Andrea last night.

B: _____

    a. Why didn't you call me and see if I wanted to go?

    b. Why did you go with Andrea and not me?

A: I did, but you weren't home.

2 *WH-* QUESTIONS IN THE SIMPLE PAST TENSE

Complete the questions. Use **was**, **were**, *or* **did**. *Then match the questions and answers.*

__e__ 1. Why _____did_____ you go there?

____ 2. Who _____ you with?

____ 3. What _____ you wear?

____ 4. How _____ the weather?

____ 5. Where _____ you yesterday?

____ 6. How _____ you get to the beach?

____ 7. Where _____ your husband?

____ 8. When _____ he come home?

____ 9. What _____ the problem with the bus?

____ 10. Why _____ he angry?

____ 11. Where _____ your friends meet you?

____ 12. Why _____ your friends late?

a. At the beach.

b. It was sunny and warm.

c. By bus.

d. It was crowded.

e. We wanted to swim.

f. Some friends.

g. At the bus station.

h. They woke up late.

i. My new bathing suit.

j. At his office.

k. He didn't go to the beach with us.

l. Late last night.

3 *WH-* QUESTIONS WITH THE PAST TENSE OF *BE*

Complete the conversations. Write correct questions.

1. **A:** Did you pay a lot of money for those sunglasses?

   B: No, they were on sale.

   A: When ___were they on sale_____?

   B: Last week.

2. **A:** I tried to call you last night.

   B: I wasn't home.

   A: Where _____?

   B: At a friend's apartment.

3. **A:** Did you have your history test yesterday?

   B: No, we had it today.

   A: How _____?

   B: It was okay, but I didn't know the answers to two of the questions.

4. **A:** Did the kids go swimming?

    B: No, they were afraid.

    A: Why _____?

    B: The water was deep.

5. **A:** Did you go to the basketball game?

    B: Yeah, it was a great game.

    A: What _____?

    B: I don't remember the score, but our team won.

6. **A:** Those are beautiful shoes. Where did you get them?

    B: At a store on Washington Street.

    A: What _____?

    B: I think the name of the store was Dalton's. Or, was it Dillon's?

7. **A:** Did your dog have her puppies yet?

    B: She sure did—six of them.

    A: When _____?

    B: They were born a few days ago.

8. **A:** What's new?

    B: The police were here.

    A: Why _____?

    B: Someone called them, but I don't know why.

9. **A:** You were brave to go there alone.

    B: I wasn't alone.

    A: Who _____?

    B: My brother and sister.

10. **A:** Did you ever read this book?

    B: Yes, it was about Eleanor Roosevelt.

    A: Who _____?

    B: She was the wife of President Roosevelt.

BE GOING TO FOR THE FUTURE; FUTURE AND PAST TIME MARKERS

1 FUTURE TIME MARKERS

Rewrite the sentences. Replace the underlined words with another future time expression. Use **tonight** *or combine the correct words from each column.*

	week
next	month
this	morning
tomorrow	afternoon
	night
	evening

(It's eleven o'clock in the morning on Wednesday, July 3rd.)

1. Keith is going to attend a meeting <u>in four hours</u>.

   Keith is going to attend a meeting this afternoon.

2. Keith and his girlfriend, Andrea, are going to visit a friend in the hospital in <u>eight hours</u>.

   _____

3. Andrea is going to go on vacation <u>in one month</u>.

   _____

4. Keith and his brother are going to play tennis <u>in twenty hours</u>.

   _____

5. Keith's brother is going to see the doctor <u>in one week</u>.

   _____

6. Keith is going to call his mother <u>in eleven hours</u>.

_____

7. Keith and Andrea are going to go to the movies <u>in thirty-four hours</u>.

_____

❷ FUTURE TIME MARKERS

Rewrite the sentences. Replace the underlined words with another future time expression. Use **in**.

(It is ten o'clock in the morning on Friday, March 5th.)

1. Richard is going to have lunch <u>at two o'clock this afternoon</u>.

   Richard is going to have lunch in four hours.

2. Richard and Irene are going to see his parents <u>on March 19th</u>.

_____

3. Irene is going to get a haircut <u>on Monday, March 8th</u>.

_____

4. Richard is going to graduate from college <u>on May 5th</u>.

_____

5. Irene is going to arrive at Richard's house <u>at 10:10 this morning</u>.

_____

❸ FUTURE PLANS

What are your plans for tomorrow? Put a check (✓) next to the things you are probably going to do. Put an **X** *next to the things you are definitely not going to do.*

_____ **1.** study

_____ **2.** go shopping

_____ **3.** take pictures

_____ **4.** watch TV

_____ **5.** go out with friends

_____ **6.** listen to music

_____ **7.** visit relatives

_____ **8.** talk on the telephone

_____ **9.** take a shower

_____ **10.** write a letter

_____ **11.** go skiing

_____ **12.** stay home

4 AFFIRMATIVE AND NEGATIVE STATEMENTS WITH *BE GOING TO*

Write six true sentences about your plans for tomorrow. Use the information from Exercise 3.

Example: ___✓___ study   ___X___ write a letter

   I am going to study tomorrow.

   I am not going to write a letter.

1. _____
2. _____
3. _____
4. _____
5. _____
6. _____

5 AFFIRMATIVE STATEMENTS WITH *BE GOING TO*

Some people are going out. What are they going to do? Make guesses and write sentences with **be going to**.

Nina is taking a tennis racket and a textbook.

1.   She's going to play tennis. _____
2. _____

Mr. and Mrs. Wu are taking paper and envelopes and skis.

3. _____
4. _____

Richard is taking CDs and a camera.

5. _____
6. _____

6 NEGATIVE STATEMENTS WITH *BE GOING TO*

Write sentences about the future. Use **not** *and* **be going to**.

1. It's Wednesday morning. Reggie usually plays tennis on Wednesday afternoon, but he has a bad cold.

   ___He isn't going to play___ tennis this afternoon.

2. It's July. Joan usually takes a vacation in August, but she has money problems this year.

   _____ a vacation this August.

3. Mary always takes a shower in the morning, but there's no hot water today.

   _____ a shower this morning.

4. It's eleven o'clock in the morning. The children usually play outside after lunch, but the weather is terrible today.

   _____ outside this afternoon.

5. It's six o'clock. Carl and his wife usually watch television after dinner, but there's nothing good on television.

   _____ television tonight.

6. It's eleven o'clock. I usually eat lunch around noon, but I finished a big breakfast at 10:30.

   _____ lunch at noon today.

7. It's twelve noon. My friend and I like to swim on Saturday afternoons, but my friend went away for the weekend and I'm tired.

   _____ this afternoon.

8. It's nine o'clock in the morning. Dr. Morita usually sees patients at his office every morning, but there's an emergency at the hospital. He can't leave until noon.

   _____ patients at his office this morning.

9. I usually wake up at six o'clock in the morning, but tomorrow is a holiday.

   _____ at six o'clock tomorrow morning.

10. It's ten o'clock in the morning. The letter carrier usually delivers all the mail by one o'clock, but he started late this morning.

    _____ all the mail by one o'clock today.

7 WH- QUESTIONS WITH *BE GOING TO*

Write questions. Use **be going to.**

1. What / he / make

_____ What is he going to make? _____

2. Who / cook / tonight

_____

3. When / dinner / be / ready

_____

4. Why / he / cook / so much food

_____

5. How long / he / need / to cook the dinner

_____

6. Who / come

_____

7. How / he / cook / the lamb

_____

8. Where / all of your guests / sit

_____

9. What / you / do

_____

10. How long / your guests / stay

_____

8 WH- QUESTIONS WITH *BE GOING TO*

Write the correct questions from Exercise 7.

1. **A:** Who's going to cook tonight?

   B: My husband.

2. **A:** _____

   B: Soup, salad, lamb, potatoes, some vegetables, and dessert.

3. **A:** _____

   B: We're going to have a dinner party.

4. **A:** _____

   B: He's going to roast it in the oven.

5. **A:** _____

   B: About fifteen of my relatives.

6. **A:** _____

   B: My husband's fast. Probably two or three hours.

7. **A:** _____

   B: I'm going to wash the dishes.

8. **A:** _____

   B: At around seven o'clock.

9. **A:** _____

   B: They're going to come at 6:00 and probably stay until about 11:00.

10. **A:** _____

    B: My sister's going to bring extra chairs.

9 PRESENT PROGRESSIVE FOR NOW AND FOR FUTURE

Underline the verb in each sentence. Write **now** *if the speaker is talking about now. Write* **future** *if the speaker is talking about the future.*

1. What <u>are</u> you <u>doing</u> tomorrow morning? _____ future _____

2. What <u>are</u> you <u>doing</u>? _____ now _____

3. I'm doing a grammar exercise. _____

4. We're not going on vacation in July. _____

5. She's leaving in two hours. _____

6. Are you doing anything special? _____

7. Is the plumber coming soon? _____

8. The students are not listening. _____

9. Where are you going this weekend? _____

10. Why is he waiting? _____

10 PRESENT PROGRESSIVE FOR FUTURE

Roger and Helen are taking a trip to Great Britain. Here is their schedule. Write sentences. Use the present progressive.

May 8	6:00 P.M. 7:30	Meet your group at the airport Fly to London
May 9	6:45 A.M.	Arrive in London
May 9 and 10		Stay at the London Regency Hotel
May 9	2:00 P.M. 4:30 7:30	Visit Buckingham Palace Have tea at the Ritz Hotel Go to the theater
May 10	9:00 A.M. 12:00 P.M.	Go on a tour of central London Eat lunch at a typical English pub
May 11	8:00 A.M.	Leave for Scotland

1. __They are meeting their group at the airport at 6:00 p.m. on May 8.__

2. _____

3. _____

4. _____

5. _____

6. _____

7. _____

8. _____

9. _____

10. _____

11 YES / NO QUESTIONS AND ANSWERS WITH THE PRESENT PROGRESSIVE FOR FUTURE

Write questions. Use the present progressive. Then answer them. Use short answers.

1. you / go / to English class / tomorrow

   __Are you going to English class tomorrow?__   Yes, I am. (OR: No, I'm not.)

2. you / go / to the movies / this weekend

   _____   _____

3. you / take a trip / next week

   _____   _____

4. your friend / leave / in two hours

   _____   _____

5. your classmates / meet you / tonight

   _____   _____

6. your mother / drive to work / tomorrow

   _____   _____

7. your father / take an English class / next year

   _____   _____

(continued on next page)

8. your neighbors / do anything / this weekend

_____   _____

9. you and your friends / play cards / next Saturday

_____   _____

10. your parents / call / your teacher / tonight

_____   _____

⑫ *WH-* QUESTIONS WITH THE PRESENT PROGRESSIVE FOR FUTURE

Ask Rosemary about her vacation plans. Write questions. Use a word
from each column and the present progressive.

Why		stay
When		take
Where		go
Who	you	go with
How long		leave
What		drive
How		get there

1. ___Where are you going?_____

To Colorado.

2. _____

On September 16th.

3. _____

By car.

4. _____

Airplane tickets are too expensive.

5. _____

Two weeks.

6. _____

Some friends from college.

7. _____

A tent, sleeping bags, and bikes.

WILL FOR THE FUTURE

1 AFFIRMATIVE STATEMENTS WITH *WILL*

Complete the conversations. Use **I'll** *and the words in the box.*

buy you some	make you a sandwich	wash them
get you some water	~~close the window~~	drive you
turn on the air conditioner	get you some aspirin	help you

1. A: I'm cold.

   B: ___I'll close the window.___

2. A: I'm thirsty.

   B: _____

3. A: I can't lift this box.

   B: _____

4. A: I need some stamps.

   B: _____

5. A: I'm hot.

   B: _____

6. A: I'm hungry.

   B: _____

7. A: I have a headache.

   B: _____

8. A: I'm late for class.

   B: _____

9. A: There are dirty dishes in the sink.

   B: _____

2 **CONTRACTIONS WITH *WILL***

Write the sentences with contractions.

1. We will meet you at 8:00. _____We'll meet you at 8:00._____

2. He will not lose his job. _____

3. I will have a cup of coffee. _____

4. It will rain this evening. _____

5. She will not be happy. _____

6. They will have a good time. _____

7. You will not like it. _____

3 **WILL VS. *BE GOING TO* VS. PRESENT PROGRESSIVE FOR FUTURE**

Complete the sentences. Circle the correct words and write them on the lines.

1. **A:** What's the weather forecast for tomorrow?

   B: The newspaper says it _____will snow_____.

   a. is snowing   **b.** will snow

2. **A:** Where are you going with the soap and water?

   B: I _____ wash the car.

   a. am going to   **b.** will

3. **A:** Do you see my umbrella?

   B: Yes, it's over there. I _____ get it for you.

   a. am going to   **b.** will

4. **A:** Why is Myra so happy these days?

   B: She _____ get married.

   a. is going to   **b.** will

5. **A:** Why _____ see that film?

   a. are you going to   **b.** will you

   B: I heard it was good.

6. A: The dishwasher isn't working. I'm going to call the repairman.

    B: No, don't. I _____ it.

        a. am fixing   **b.** will fix

7. A: I think men _____ dresses in the future.

        a. are wearing   **b.** will wear

    B: You're crazy!

8. A: _____ anything this weekend?

        a. Are you doing   **b.** Will you do

    B: I'm not sure yet. Why?

9. A: _____ everything by computer in fifty years?

        a. Are people buying   **b.** Will people buy

    B: Maybe.

❹ NEGATIVE STATEMENTS WITH *WILL*

Write negative sentences with the same meaning.

1. The car will be small.

    The car won't be big.

2. I'll leave early.

    _____

3. It'll be cold.

    _____

4. Coffee will cost less.

    _____

5. The dishes will be clean.

    _____

(continued on next page)

6. We will come after seven o'clock.

_____

7. Mr. and Mrs. McNamara will buy an old car.

_____

8. I'll make a few eggs.

_____

9. Valerie will win the game.

_____

10. The parking lot will be empty.

_____

5 AFFIRMATIVE AND NEGATIVE STATEMENTS AND YES / NO AND WH- QUESTIONS WITH WILL

*A fortune teller is telling Mark about his future. Complete the conversation. Use **will** or **won't** and the words in parentheses.*

FORTUNE TELLER: Your future _____ will be _____ a happy one.
1. (be)

MARK: _____ rich?
2. (I / be)

FORTUNE TELLER: Yes. You _____ a very rich woman.
3. (marry)

MARK: Where _____ her?
4. (I / meet)

FORTUNE TELLER: That I can't tell you, but it _____ love at first
5. (be)

sight.

MARK: _____ me forever?
6. (she / love)

FORTUNE TELLER: Forever.

MARK: When _____?
7. (we / meet)

FORTUNE TELLER: Soon.

MARK: What about children?

FORTUNE TELLER: You _____ many children—just two, a boy
8. (not have)

and a girl.

MARK: That's a good number. What else?

FORTUNE TELLER: You _____ famous.
9. (be)

MARK: Really? Why _____ famous?
10. (I / be)

FORTUNE TELLER: I'm not sure, but it _____ fun for you.
11. (not be)

People _____ you all the time.
12. (bother)

MARK: Oh! I _____ that.
13. (not like)

_____ everything?
14. (our home / have)

FORTUNE TELLER: Yes, everything.

MARK: Good. Then we _____ it, and
15. (not leave)

people _____ us.
16. (not bother)

FORTUNE TELLER: But then you _____ a prisoner in you own
17. (become)

home. _____ you happy?
18. (that / make)

MARK: Oh, why isn't life perfect?

FORTUNE TELLER: That I cannot tell you.

UNIT

COUNT AND NON-COUNT NOUNS AND QUANTIFIERS

1 COUNT NOUNS VS. NON-COUNT NOUNS

Look at the store signs. Write the correct aisle number.

1	4	7
Eggs Butter Juice Cheese Milk	Toilet Paper Paper Towels Napkins Plastic Bags	Frozen Food Ice Cream

2	5	8
Bread Rolls	Potato Chips Cookies Cereal	Canned Vegetables Canned Fish Rice

3	6	9
Toothbrushes Toothpaste Soap Shampoo	Sugar Flour Salt	Fresh Fruit

1. Sugar is in aisle __6__.

2. Cookies are in aisle ____.

3. Ice cream is in aisle ____.

4. Eggs are in aisle ____.

5. Fruit is in aisle ____.

6. Canned vegetables are in aisle ____.

7. Napkins are in aisle ____.

8. Milk is in aisle ____.

9. Rice is in aisle ____.

10. Plastic bags are in aisle ____.

11. Potato chips are in aisle ____.

12. Frozen food is in aisle ____.

13. Bread is in aisle ____.

14. Canned fish is in aisle ____.

15. Toothbrushes are in aisle ____.

② COUNT NOUNS VS. NON-COUNT NOUNS

Write the underlined words in Exercise 1 in the correct column.

Count Nouns	Non-Count Nouns
cookies	sugar

③ COUNT NOUNS VS. NON-COUNT NOUNS

*Circle the twelve words that don't belong in the lists of count nouns and non-count nouns. Then write correct lists. Write **a**, **an**, or **some** before each word.*

Count Nouns	Non-Count Nouns	Count Nouns	Non-Count Nouns
egg	(books)	an egg	some bread
(bread)	food	some books	some food
furniture	water		
student	people		
money	paper		
information	uncle		
teeth	homework		
rain	advice		
children	television		
friends	traffic		
oil	questions		
animal	computer		

4 COUNT NOUNS VS. NON-COUNT NOUNS

Complete the sentences. Circle the correct answers and write them on the lines.

1. Do you have _____ a pencil _____?

   a. some pencil

   (b.) a pencil

2. The _____ on the table.

   a. money is

   b. money are

3. There _____ in the refrigerator.

   a. is some milk

   b. are some milks

4. We don't have _____.

   a. much book

   b. many books

5. Do you want _____?

   a. a magazine

   b. some magazine

6. I'm sorry I'm late. The _____ terrible.

   a. traffic was

   b. traffics were

7. Do you like Chinese _____?

   a. food

   b. foods

8. Do you have _____?

   a. a water

   b. any water

9. Is there _____ in the bedroom?

   a. a radio

   b. any radio

10. Don't rush! We have a lot of _____.

    a. time

    b. times

11. I want _____.

    a. an information

    b. some information

5 **A VS. *THE***

*Complete the conversations. Use **a** or **the**.*

1. **A:** _____The_____ food is very good.

   B: Thanks. There's more in _____the_____ kitchen.

2. **A:** What would you like to drink?

   B: _____ cup of coffee, please.

3. **A:** How did you get here?

   B: I took _____ subway.

4. **A:** What are you doing?

   B: I'm listening to _____ radio.

5. **A:** Do you have _____ car?

   B: No, but I'd like to buy one.

6. **A:** What is _____ capital of the United States?

   B: Washington, D.C. It's _____ pretty big city.

7. **A:** How did you do on _____ test?

   B: Okay, but I wasn't sure about _____ last part.

8. **A:** Look! Here's _____ postcard from Suzanne.

   B: That's _____ beautiful picture. Where is she?

6 **SOME VS. ANY VS. A**

*Jack went shopping. He didn't buy everything on his shopping list, but he crossed out the things he bought. Write sentences about what he did and didn't buy. Use **some**, **any**, or **a**.*

```
┌─────────────────────────────────┐
│        Shopping List            │
│                                 │
│   B̶a̶n̶a̶n̶a̶s̶       Toothbrush       │
│                                 │
│   Cheese        P̶o̶t̶a̶t̶o̶e̶s̶         │
│                                 │
│   O̶r̶a̶n̶g̶e̶ ̶j̶u̶i̶c̶e̶   Lettuce         │
│                                 │
│   Lemons        Carrots         │
│                                 │
│   N̶e̶w̶s̶p̶a̶p̶e̶r̶      B̶u̶t̶t̶e̶r̶          │
│                                 │
│   Bread         M̶i̶l̶k̶            │
│                                 │
│   Onions        E̶g̶g̶s̶            │
└─────────────────────────────────┘
```

1. He bought some bananas.

2. He didn't buy any cheese.

3. _____

4. _____

5. _____

6. _____

7. _____

8. _____

9. _____

10. _____

11. _____

12. _____

13. _____

14. _____

7 COUNT AND NON-COUNT NOUN QUANTIFIERS

Write true sentences. Choose words from each column.

I have	a lot of a little a few	cheese in my pocket food in my refrigerator money in my pocket books next to my bed shirts in my closet friends free time
I don't have	much many any	children work to do today questions for my teacher jewelry medicine in my bathroom problems with English grammar photographs in my wallet ice cream at home

1.   I don't have any cheese in my pocket.

2. _____

3. _____

4. _____

5. _____

6. _____

7. _____

8. _____

9. _____

10. _____

QUESTIONS WITH *ANY / SOME / HOW MUCH / HOW MANY*; QUANTIFIERS; CONTAINERS

1 CONTAINERS AND NON-COUNT NOUNS

Match the containers and non-count nouns.

_b_	**1.** a can of	**a.**	lettuce
____	**2.** a carton of	**b.**	soda
____	**3.** a head of	**c.**	bread
____	**4.** a loaf of	**d.**	milk

Do the same with these words.

____	**5.** a bottle of	**e.**	cake
____	**6.** a box of	**f.**	cigarettes
____	**7.** a pack of	**g.**	juice
____	**8.** a piece of	**h.**	cereal

Do the same with these words, too.

____	**9.** a bar of	**i.**	toothpaste
____	**10.** a jar of	**j.**	toilet paper
____	**11.** a roll of	**k.**	jam
____	**12.** a tube of	**l.**	soap

2 QUESTIONS WITH *HOW MUCH* AND *HOW MANY* AND CONTAINERS

Look at Tina's cash register receipt and answer the questions.

```
6 Soda              $2.19
1 Bread             $1.05
1 Milk              $1.19
2 Lettuce           $3.58
3 Apple juice       $5.40
1 Cereal            $2.29
4 Toilet paper      $1.69
3 Soap              $2.45
1 Toothpaste        $2.39
2 Jam               $3.38
        TOTAL      $25.61

   THANK YOU FOR SHOPPING
        AT CASTLE'S
```

1. How much soda did she buy?

   _Six cans._____

2. How many loaves of bread did she buy?

   _One._____

3. How much milk did she buy?

   _____

4. How much lettuce did she buy?

   _____

5. How many bottles of apple juice did she

   buy? _____

6. How many boxes of cereal did she buy?

   _____

7. How much toilet paper did she buy?

   _____

8. How much soap did she buy?

   _____

9. How much toothpaste did she buy?

   _____

10. How many jars of jam did she buy?

   _____

3 YES / NO QUESTIONS WITH COUNT AND NON-COUNT NOUNS

Write questions. Use **a**, **an**, *or* **any**. *Then answer the questions with short answers.*

1. telephone / in your bedroom

   Is there a telephone in your bedroom?   Yes, there is. (OR: No, there isn't.)

2. plants / in your home

   Are there any plants in your home?   Yes, there is. (OR: No, there isn't.)

3. trash / in your kitchen

   Is there any trash in your kitchen?   Yes, there is. (OR: No, there isn't.)

4. furniture / in your home

   _____   _____

5. clothes / in your closet

   _____   _____

6. money / under your bed

   _____   _____

7. alarm clock / next to your bed

   _____   _____

8. snow / outside your home

   _____   _____

9. sink / in your bathroom

   _____   _____

10. dishes / in your kitchen sink

    _____   _____

11. pictures / in your bedroom

    _____   _____

12. candy / in your home

    _____   _____

13. window / in your kitchen

_____   _____

14. television / in your living room

_____   _____

4 **QUESTIONS WITH *HOW MUCH* AND *HOW MANY***

Complete the conversation. Write questions using **how much** *or* **how many**.

A: Are you going to the store?

B: Yes, why?

A: I need some things. I need some cheese.

B: How much cheese do you need? _____
                                  1.

A: About a pound. And I want some eggs.

B: How many eggs do you want? _____
                                 2.

A: A dozen. I also need some flour.

B: _____
       3.

A: One pound, I think.

B: Do you want any sugar?

A: No, I have sugar.

B: _____
       4.

A: I have a few cups, at least. But I want some bananas.

B: _____
       5.

A: Five or six. I want some oranges, too.

B: _____
       6.

A: A few. Oh, and I need some cereal.

B: _____
       7.

(continued on next page)

A: Just one box. I also need some potatoes.

B: _____
8.

A: Get about ten. Oh, one more thing. I want some milk.

B: _____
9.

A: Half a gallon. Oh, don't forget to get some flowers. I want roses.

B: _____
10.

A: Half a dozen.

B: Is that it? Are you sure you don't want any cookies?

A: No, I have enough cookies.

B: _____
11.

A: Two dozen. Here, let me give you some money.

B: I have money.

A: _____
12.

B: About twenty dollars.

A: Here. Take another twenty.

5 TOO MUCH, TOO MANY, AND *NOT ENOUGH*

Write sentences about the pictures. Use **too much**, **too many**, *or* **not enough** *and the words in the box.*

air	birds	days	furniture	~~people~~	toothpaste
batteries	chairs	food	numbers	shampoo	water

1.

__There are too many__

__people in the boat.__

2.

_____

_____

3.

_____

_____

4.

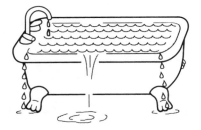

_____

_____

5.

_____

_____

6.

_____

_____

7.

_____

_____

8.

_____

_____

9.

_____

_____

(continued on next page)

10.

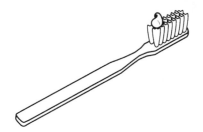

_____

_____

11.

_____

_____

12.

_____

_____

6 TOO LITTLE AND TOO FEW

Rewrite the sentences. Use **too little** *or* **too few**.

1. We don't have enough chairs.

   We have too few chairs.

2. There isn't enough salt in this soup.

   There's too little salt in this soup.

3. There weren't enough people for two teams.

_____

4. We didn't have enough paper for everyone in the class.

_____

5. There wasn't enough food for fifteen people.

_____

6. You don't have enough information.

_____

7. There aren't enough bedrooms in that apartment.

_____

8. We didn't have enough time for the test.

_____

9. These aren't enough bananas for a banana cake.

_____

10. There aren't enough sales clerks at that store.

_____

7 REVIEW OF QUANTIFIERS

Complete the sentences. Circle the correct answers and write them on the lines.

1. What did the student say to the teacher?

"I didn't finish the homework. I _____ didn't have enough _____ time."

  a. had too much

  (b.) didn't have enough

2. What did the driver say to the passenger?

"We _____ gas. We need to go to the gas station."

  a. have too much

  b. don't have enough

3. What did the passenger say to the driver?

"There _____ cars. Let's go to another parking lot."

  a. are too many

  b. aren't enough

4. What did the cashier say to the child?

"I'm sorry. You have _____ money. Go home and get some more."

  a. too much

  b. too little

(continued on next page)

5. Ted and Niki wanted to see a movie, but there was a long line for tickets. What did

   Ted say?

   "There are _____ people. Let's see another movie."

   a. too many

   b. too few

6. What did the doctor say to the patient?

   "You said you're on a diet, but you lost only one pound last month. That

   _____ weight."

   a. is too much

   b. isn't enough

7. What did the photography teacher say to the student?

   "This picture is dark. You had _____ light."

   a. too much

   b. too little

8. What did Mitchell's mother say to him?

   "You ate _____ fruit. That's why you have a stomachache."

   a. too much

   b. too little

9. What did the customer say to the waitress?

   "There are _____ forks on the table for six people. Please

   bring some more."

   a. too many

   b. too few

10. What did Debbie say to her roommate?

   "You bought _____ juice. There's no place to put all these

   bottles."

   a. too much

   b. too little

CAN AND COULD FOR ABILITY AND POSSIBILITY; MAY I, CAN I, AND COULD I FOR POLITE REQUESTS

 ABILITY

Look at the job advertisements. Look at the qualifications of Martha, Frank, Les, and Rosa. Then answer the questions.

WANTED
SECRETARY
Type 70 words per minute.
Need to speak Spanish.

WANTED
SUMMER BABYSITTER
Take two small children to the beach every day. Also, go horseback riding with ten-year-old girl.

DRIVER WANTED
Drive truck to airport every day. Pick up boxes and deliver to downtown offices.

WANTED
SUMMER CAMP WORKER
◆ Teach children the guitar
◆ Also work with children in art class

	Martha	Frank	Les	Rosa
draw	no	no	yes	yes
drive	yes	no	yes	no
lift 100 pounds	no	no	yes	yes
play the guitar	no	yes	no	yes
ride a horse	yes	no	no	no
speak Spanish	no	yes	no	yes
swim	yes	yes	no	yes
type	yes	yes	no	no

1. Which job is good for Martha? The job as a ____summer babysitter____.

2. Which job is good for Frank? The job as a _____.

3. Which job is good for Les? The job as a _____.

4. Which job is good for Rosa? The job as a _____.

❷ AFFIRMATIVE AND NEGATIVE STATEMENTS WITH *CAN* FOR ABILITY

Look at the information in Exercise 1 again. Then answer the questions.
Use **can** *or* **can't**.

1. Why is the job as babysitter good for Martha?

   She ___can swim and ride a horse.___

2. Why isn't the job as babysitter good for Rosa?

   She ___can swim, but she can't ride a horse.___

3. Why isn't the job as babysitter good for Les?

   He ___can't swim, and he can't ride a horse.___

4. Why is the job as driver good for Les?

   He _____

5. Why is the job as secretary good for Frank?

   He _____

6. Why is the job as summer camp worker good for Rosa?

   She _____

7. Why isn't the job as driver good for Frank?

   He _____

8. Why isn't the job as secretary good for Martha?

   She _____

9. Why isn't the job as driver good for Rosa?

   She _____

10. Why isn't the job as summer camp worker good for Les?

    He _____

11. Why isn't the job as summer camp worker good for Martha?

    She _____

12. Why isn't the job as secretary good for Les?

    He _____

3 YES / NO QUESTIONS WITH *CAN*

Write questions. Use **can**. *Then answer the questions. Use short answers.*

1. you / drive

_____Can you drive?_____   _____Yes, I can. (OR: No, I can't.)_____

2. your mother / lift 100 pounds

_____   _____

3. your father / play the guitar

_____   _____

4. your best friend / ride a horse

_____   _____

5. your parents / speak Spanish

_____   _____

6. you / swim

_____   _____

7. you / type

_____   _____

4 AFFIRMATIVE AND NEGATIVE STATEMENTS WITH *COULD* FOR PAST ABILITY

Complete the sentences. Use **could** *or* **couldn't** *and the verbs in parentheses.*

1. I'm sorry that I _____couldn't call_____ you yesterday. I was very busy.
          (call)

2. We enjoyed our holiday in Spain because we _____ our
          Spanish.   **(practice)**

3. We (go) _____ to the party last night. Our son was ill.
          (go)

4. I didn't answer the questions. I _____ the story.
                              (understand)

(continued on next page)

5. I had a terrible stomachache yesterday. I _____ a thing.
   (eat)

6. In high school I had a lot of free time. I _____ soccer with
   (play)
   my friends every Saturday and Sunday.

7. We didn't meet our friends for dinner last night. We _____
   (find)
   the restaurant.

8. Our room in that hotel was terrible. We _____ the people in
   (hear)
   the other rooms all the time.

9. Last weekend, we stayed indoors. It was very cold, and we _____
   (go)
   outside.

10. I liked my summer vacation. I _____ whatever I wanted.
    (do)

5 MAY AND *CAN* FOR POLITE REQUESTS

Make polite requests. Use **may I** *or* **can I**.

1. You have a doctor's appointment at four o'clock. You want to leave early because class
   finishes at four o'clock. Ask your teacher.

   Can I leave class early? (OR: May I leave class early?)

2. You're in a friend's room. You're hot and you want to open the window. Ask your friend.

   _____

3. You're in an office. You want to use the telephone on the secretary's desk. Ask the
   secretary.

   _____

4. Your classmate has a car, but you don't have one. It's raining, and you want to get a
   ride. Ask your classmate.

   _____

5. You made a mistake. You don't have an eraser, but your classmate has an eraser. Ask
   your classmate.

   _____

6. You're at your neighbor's house. You want to have a drink of water. Ask your neighbor.

_____

7. You have a question about something in your grammar book. Ask your teacher.

_____

8. You're at a restaurant. You want to sit at the empty table in the corner. Ask the waiter.

_____

36 MAY OR *MIGHT* FOR POSSIBILITY

1 MAY FOR PERMISSION AND POSSIBILITY

Write **permission** *if the speaker is giving, refusing, or asking for permission. Write* **possibility** *if the speaker is talking about possibility.*

1. Don't call Carol. She may be asleep. _____possibility_____

2. It's noisy outside. May I close the window? _____permission_____

3. You may not talk during the test. _____

4. The government may raise taxes. _____

5. Lie down. You may feel better. _____

6. You may enter that room of the old house, but be careful. _____

7. Some of the students may not do the homework. _____

8. May my roommate come to the party, too? _____

9. The mailman is coming. There may be a letter for me. _____

10. Nobody may leave before eleven o'clock. _____

2 MAY AND *MIGHT* FOR POSSIBILITY

Rewrite the sentences. Use **may** *or* **might**.

1. Maybe it will snow.

   It may snow. (OR: It might snow.)

2. Perhaps we'll come by taxi.

   _____

3. Perhaps he won't want to come.

   _____

4. Maybe they'll study.

_____

5. Perhaps the store will be closed.

_____

6. Maybe she won't finish the work by Friday.

_____

7. Maybe the dog will come home.

_____

8. Perhaps you won't like that kind of food.

_____

9. Maybe I won't leave before seven o'clock.

_____

10. Perhaps the cookies won't taste good.

_____

3 WILL FOR DEFINITE FUTURE VS. MAY FOR POSSIBILITY

Complete the sentences. Use **may** *or* **will**.

1. Tomorrow is my birthday. I _____will_____ be twenty-five.

2. I'm tall. My children _____may_____ be tall, too.

3. I don't know anything about that movie. It _____ not be good.

4. Are you taking a trip to the United States? You _____ need a passport. Everybody from Brazil needs one.

5. Don't worry. I _____ do it. I promise.

6. Ask about the price. It _____ be expensive.

7. The supermarket _____ sell flowers, but I'm not sure.

8. There's someone at the door. I _____ open it.

9. The sun _____ rise tomorrow.

10. The food _____ be ready. I'm going to look.

4 AFFIRMATIVE AND NEGATIVE STATEMENTS WITH *MAY* AND *MIGHT*

Complete the sentences. Use **may (not)** *or* **might (not)** *and the words in the box.*

bite	close	get lost	have an accident	~~pass~~
break	~~fall~~	get sick	live	win

1. Janet is worried about her little boy. He's climbing a tree.

   He ___may fall. (OR: might fall.)___

2. Jimmy has a test today, and he didn't study.

   He ___may not pass. (OR: might not pass.)___

3. Lynn is driving fast.

   She _____

4. Wrap those glasses carefully.

   They _____

5. Mark Muller is one of the top tennis players in the world, but he isn't playing well today.

   He _____

6. Don't lose these directions. It's difficult to find my house.

   You _____

7. The woman's injuries are very bad.

   She _____

8. Don't go near that animal.

   It _____

9. Don't go outside with wet hair. It's cold.

   You _____

10. That store never has many customers.

    It _____

DESIRES, INVITATIONS, REQUESTS: WOULD LIKE, WOULD YOU LIKE . . . ?, WOULD YOU PLEASE . . . ?

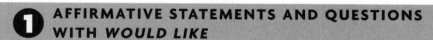

① AFFIRMATIVE STATEMENTS AND QUESTIONS WITH *WOULD LIKE*

Read each conversation. Then answer the question.

Conversation A

A: Can I help you?
B: Yes, I'd like two tickets to Pittsburgh.
A: Would you like one-way or round-trip?
B: Round-trip, please.
A: That's $38.90.
B: Here you are. What time is the next bus?
A: At 9:30.
B: Thank you.

1. Where does Conversation A take place?

_____

Conversation B

A: Sir, would you like chicken or fish?
B: Chicken, please.
A: And what would you like to drink?
B: Just some water, please.
A: And your wife?
B: She doesn't want anything. She doesn't like airplane food.

2. Where does Conversation B take place?

_____

Conversation C

A: Where would you like to sit?
B: These seats are fine. I don't want to sit too close to the screen.
A: Would you like some popcorn?
B: No, but I'd like something to drink. But hurry! The movie's going to start.

3. Where does Conversation C take place?

_____

❷ AFFIRMATIVE STATEMENTS AND *YES / NO* QUESTIONS WITH *WOULD LIKE*

Rewrite the sentences. Use **would like**.

1. I want two airmail stamps.

   _____I would like two airmail stamps._____

2. Do you want to have dinner with me?

   _____Would you like to have dinner with me?_____

3. Sheila wants to talk to you.

   _____

4. Do your parents want to come?

   _____

5. Sandy and Billy want some coffee.

   _____

6. Does Dan want to come with us?

   _____

7. My friend and I want a table for two.

   _____

8. Does the teacher want to come to the party?

   _____

9. I want to take a long trip.

   _____

10. We want you to have dinner with us.

   _____

3 WOULD LIKE + OBJECT + INFINITIVE

Ari is planning a surprise birthday party for his roommate, Tony. He needs help from his friends. Look at his list. Write sentences. Use **would like**.

Surprise Birthday Party

Jerry—do some of the shopping

Conchita—bring the CDs

Irene and Amira—help with the cooking

Eric—bring his CD player

Harry, Mike, and Tom—move the furniture

Ellen—buy some ice cream

Victor—pick up the birthday cake

Carmen and Ted—keep Tony busy

Ratana—make the decorations

---

1. Ari would like Jerry to do some of the shopping.

2. _____

3. _____

4. _____

5. _____

6. _____

7. _____

8. _____

9. _____

4 STATEMENTS AND QUESTIONS WITH *WOULD LIKE*

Complete the conversation. Use the words in parentheses.

DAVE: Hi, Ellen. Come on in.

ELLEN: Hi, Dave. Thanks.

DAVE: _____Would you like_____ some coffee?
             1. (you / like)

ELLEN: Yes. That sounds good. _____ some help?
                                    2. (you / like)

DAVE: No, it's ready. Here you are.

ELLEN: Thanks.

DAVE: _____ some cookies, too?
           3. (you / like)

ELLEN: No, thanks, but I _____ some sugar for my coffee.
                              4. (like)

DAVE: Oh, sorry. I forgot. Here's the sugar.

ELLEN: Boy, it's cold outside.

DAVE: _____ you a sweater?
           5. (you / like / me / give)

ELLEN: No, I'm okay.

DAVE: So, _____ this evening?
              6. (what / you / like / do)

ELLEN: I don't know. _____?
                          7. (Where / you / like / go)

DAVE: _____ to the movies?
           8. (you / like / go)

ELLEN: What's playing?

DAVE: *Forever Love* is at the Rex. _____ that?
                                        9. (you / like / see)

ELLEN: Okay. What time does it start?

DAVE: We can go at six, eight, or ten.

ELLEN: I don't care. _____?
                          10. (What time / you / like / go)

DAVE: Eight is fine, but I _____ something to eat
                               11. (like / get)

   first.

ELLEN: Okay. _____?
                  12. (Where / you / like / eat)

DAVE: How about John's Pizzeria?

ELLEN: That sounds good.

⑤ *WOULD* AND *COULD* FOR POLITE REQUESTS

Write correct questions. Use **please** *with* **would you** *or* **could you**.

1. Ask a stranger on the bus to tell you the time.

   Would you please tell me the time? (OR: Could you please tell me the time?)

2. Ask a desk clerk at a hotel to give you the key to your room.

_____

3. Ask your teacher to explain the meaning of the word *grateful*.

_____

4. Ask a cashier to give you change for a dollar.

_____

5. Ask a stranger to take a picture of you and your friends.

_____

6. Ask a taxi driver to take you to the airport.

_____

7. Ask a neighbor to help you with your suitcases.

_____

8. Ask a sales clerk to show you the brown shoes in the window.

_____

9. Ask the person in front of you at a basketball game to sit down.

_____

UNIT 38

COMPARATIVE FORM OF ADJECTIVES

1 COMPARATIVE FORM OF ADJECTIVES

Put a check (✓) next to the statements that are true. (Look at your Student Book if you need help.)

_____ **1.** Carol is neater than Yoko is.

_____ **2.** Lulu is older than Pete is.

_____ **3.** Doug is younger than Carol is.

_____ **4.** Carol is more hardworking than Norma is.

_____ **5.** Yoko is more interested in her studies than Carol is.

_____ **6.** Lulu is busier than Pete is.

_____ **7.** Yoko is farther from home than Carol is.

2 COMPARATIVE FORM OF ADJECTIVES

Put the words in the box in the correct columns.

~~big~~	difficult	heavy	messy
~~careful~~	easy	high	noisy
~~comfortable~~	expensive	hot	old
crowded	fast	intelligent	pretty
dangerous	friendly	long	small

One Syllable	Two Syllables	Three or Four Syllables
big	careful	comfortable

③ COMPARATIVE FORM OF ADJECTIVES

Complete the sentences. Use the comparative form of the adjectives.

1. That car is old, but this car is ___older_____.

2. That book is good, but this book is _____.

3. The train station is far, but the airport is _____.

4. Tom is intelligent, but his brother is _____.

5. The service at that restaurant is bad, but the food is _____.

6. My sister's messy, but my brother is _____.

7. This chair is comfortable, but that chair is _____.

8. My husband is careful, but his father is _____.

9. This picture is pretty, but that picture is _____.

10. Chemistry is difficult, but physics is _____.

11. This exercise is easy, but the last exercise was _____.

④ COMPARATIVE FORM OF ADJECTIVES

Complete the sentences with the correct adjectives. Use the comparative form of the adjectives in parentheses and **than**.

1. San Francisco is _____smaller than_____ New York.
   (big / small)

2. The Nile River is _____ the Mississippi River.
   (long / short)

3. A Mercedes is _____ a Volkswagen.
   (cheap / expensive)

4. An ocean is _____ a lake.
   (big / small)

5. Mountains are _____ hills.
   (low / high)

6. Egypt is _____ Canada.
   (cold / hot)

7. Skiing is _____ golf.
   (safe / dangerous)

(continued on next page)

8. Cities are _____ villages.
   (crowded / empty)

9. Cars are _____ bicycles.
   (noisy / quiet)

10. A rock is _____ a leaf.
    (heavy / light)

11. Rabbits are _____ snails.
    (slow / fast)

12. Dogs are _____ wolves.
    (friendly / unfriendly)

5 COMPARATIVE FORM OF ADJECTIVES

Write questions. Use the comparative form of the adjectives. Then answer the questions.

1. Carol / neat / or / messy / Yoko

   _____Is Carol neater or messier than Yoko?_____   _____Carol is messier._____

2. this unit / easy / or / difficult / the last unit

   _____   _____

3. this watch / cheap / or / expensive / that watch

   _____   _____

4. you / young / or / old / your best friend

   _____   _____

5. you / tall / or / short / your teacher

   _____   _____

6. your hometown / big / or / small / Los Angeles

   _____   _____

7. today's weather / good / or / bad / yesterday's weather

   _____   _____

ADVERBS OF MANNER AND COMPARATIVE FORMS OF ADVERBS

1 ADJECTIVES VS. ADVERBS

*Write **adjective** if the underlined word is an adjective. Write **adverb** if it is an adverb.*

1. Norma works <u>hard</u>. _____adverb_____

2. Carol's room is <u>dirty</u>. _____adjective_____

3. Pete drives <u>slowly</u>. _____

4. This exercise isn't <u>hard</u>. _____

5. Everyone's going to come <u>early</u>. _____

6. Carol did <u>badly</u> on the test. _____

7. Don't drive <u>fast</u>. _____

8. The food smells <u>good</u>. _____

9. That shirt is <u>ugly</u>. _____

10. I want to speak English <u>fluently</u>. _____

11. Carry these glasses <u>carefully</u>. _____

12. I was <u>tired</u> yesterday. _____

❷ ADVERBS OF MANNER

Circle the ten adverbs in the box.

```
B   H   A   P   P   I   L   Y   F   A   X   M
A   E   A   S   I   L   Y   Q   A   X   D   O
D   A   N   G   E   R   O   U   S   L   Y   S
L   V   G   X   X   C   X   I   T   E   X   X
Y   I   R   P   A   T   I   E   N   T   L   Y
X   L   I   A   F   X   X   T   O   C   X   D
E   Y   L   S   W   E   L   L   B   N   O   R
X   X   Y   N   X   N   L   Y   I   K   X   E
```

❸ ADVERBS OF MANNER

Complete the sentences. Use the adverbs in Exercise 2.

1. It's snowing _____heavily_____. We can't drive in this weather.

2. Please talk _____. The baby's sleeping.

3. Vinny drives _____. One day he's going to have an accident.

4. Lenore was an hour late for class. Her teacher looked at her _____.

5. The children played with their toys _____.

6. She plays the guitar very _____. Everyone loves to listen to her.

7. I never eat my father's food. He cooks _____.

8. I can't understand him. He speaks _____.

9. I waited _____, but the doctor never came.

10. Your directions were very good. I found the restaurant _____.

4 ADJECTIVES VS. ADVERBS

Complete the conversations. Use the adjectives in the box or their adverb forms.

angry	easy	loud
beautiful	fast	~~quiet~~
careful	good	tired

1. **A:** Shh! Be _____ quiet _____! The baby's sleeping.

   B: Okay. I'll open the door _____ quietly _____.

2. **A:** The flowers are _____.

   B: They smell _____, too.

3. **A:** Is Gerry a _____ eater?

   B: Yes, she eats very _____. She always finishes dinner before me.

4. **A:** You look _____.

   B: I am _____. I'm going to bed.

5. **A:** Did Samara do _____ on the test?

   B: Yes. She got an A. She's a _____ student.

6. **A:** Does your daughter drive _____?

   B: Oh, yes. She's a very _____ driver. I never worry about her.

7. **A:** The music in that apartment is always _____.

   B: You're right. They play their music very _____.

8. **A:** Why did she leave the room so _____?

   B: I'm not sure. I think she was _____ with her boss.

9. **A:** That was an _____ test.

   B: I agree. I answered all the questions very _____.

5 COMPARATIVE FORMS OF ADVERBS

Complete the conversations. Use the comparative form of the adverb.

1. **A:** Did Ruben come early?

   B: Yes, but I came _____ *earlier* _____ .

2. **A:** Does Alejandro work hard?

   B: Yes, but En Mi works _____ .

3. **A:** Did your team play well?

   B: Yes, but the other team played _____ .

4. **A:** Does Andrew type carefully?

   B: Yes, but Brian types _____ .

5. **A:** Did the waiter yesterday serve you fast?

   B: Yes, but the waiter last week served us _____ .

6. **A:** Does Adam write neatly?

   B: Yes, but his sister writes _____ .

7. **A:** Does your husband dance badly?

   B: Yes, but I dance _____ .

8. **A:** Does the mechanic on Elm Street fix cars quickly?

   B: Yes, but the mechanic on Diamond Street fixes them _____ .

9. **A:** Did you learn to ride a bike easily?

   B: Yes, but my younger brother learned _____ .

10. **A:** Can you jump high?

    B: Yes, but Charlie can jump _____ .

11. **A:** Did the cashier speak to you rudely?

    B: Yes, but the manager spoke to me _____ .

ADJECTIVE + ENOUGH / TOO / VERY; AS + ADJECTIVE / ADVERB + AS

1 TOO AND ENOUGH

Match the questions and answers.

1. __b__ What's wrong with the soup?

2. ____ Do you want to go to that restaurant?

3. ____ Can you hear the music?

4. ____ Why are they playing baseball without you?

5. ____ Do you like boxing?

6. ____ Are you going to wear that dress?

7. ____ Do you drive?

8. ____ Are you happy with your grade on the test?

    a. No, it's too violent.

    b. It's too salty.

    c. I'm not good enough.

    d. No, it's too tight.

    e. No, I'm not old enough

    f. No, it's too crowded.

    g. No, it isn't high enough.

    h. No, the radio's not loud enough.

2 TOO + ADJECTIVE

Rewrite the sentences. Use **too**.

1. The bathing suit isn't dry enough to wear.

      The bathing suit is too wet to wear.

2. The apartment isn't big enough for six people.

   _____

3. Shirley and Jack aren't fast enough to run in the race.

   _____

4. The car isn't cheap enough to buy.

   _____

(continued on next page)

5. The children aren't old enough to start school.

_____

6. The room isn't warm enough.

_____

3 ADJECTIVE + *NOT ENOUGH*

Rewrite the sentences. Use **not enough**.

1. It's too cold to sit outside.

   It isn't warm enough to sit outside.

2. The jacket is too small for me.

_____

3. The break was too short.

_____

4. It's too dark to take a picture.

_____

5. It's too noisy to talk.

_____

6. Buses are too slow.

_____

4 TOO AND *VERY*

Complete the sentences. Use **too** *or* **very**.

1. A: Do you like my new dress?

   B: Yes, it's _____*very*_____ pretty.

2. A: Put these sweaters in the drawer.

   B: I can't. The drawer's _____ full.

3. A: Mommy, I want to swim in the baby pool.

   B: You're _____ big. You're not a baby.

4. A: What do you think of that hotel?

   B: The rooms are _____ nice, but it's expensive.

5. A: How's the weather in Montreal in January?

   B: It's _____ cold.

6. A: Can you read that sign?

   B: No, it's _____ far away.

7. A: Are you going to buy the stereo?

   B: I think so. The price is _____ good.

8. A: The floor's _____ dirty.

   B: I'll wash it.

9. A: Put this bag in your pocket.

   B: I can't. It's _____ big.

---

5 TOO OR *ENOUGH* + INFINITIVE

Combine the sentences. Use **too** *or* **enough** *and an infinitive.*

1. I can't watch the movie. It's too sad.

   The movie is too sad to watch.

2. I can't drink this coffee. It's too strong.

   _____

3. Pete did not understand the instructions. They were too difficult.

   _____

4. We can't eat the fruit. It's not ripe enough.

   _____

5. We can't wait. The line's too long.

   _____

6. She didn't wash the sweater by hand. It was too dirty.

   _____

(continued on next page)

7. You can't marry him. He's not rich enough.

_____

8. You can eat the eggs. They're cooked enough.

_____

6 TOO, ENOUGH, AND NOT ENOUGH

Complete the conversations. Use **too***,* **enough***, or* **not enough** *and the adjective in parentheses.*

1. A: Why did you take the pants back to the store?

   B: They were _____ too long _____. I exchanged them for a shorter pair.
   (long)

2. A: Do you want me to wash the car again?

   B: Yes. It's _____ not clean enough _____.
   (clean)

3. A: Let's go into that big old house. I want to see what's in there.

   B: No, I'm _____. There may be ghosts.
   (frightened)

4. A: Are the shoes comfortable?

   B: No, they're _____. I need a size 8, and they're a size 7.
   (big)

5. A: Why didn't you get the tickets?

   B: It was _____. There weren't any left.
   (late)

6. A: Is the soup _____?
   (hot)
   B: Yeah. Thanks for heating it up.

7. A: How are the pants?

   B: They're _____. I think I need a larger size.
   (tight)

8. A: Why do I need to rewrite this composition?

   B: Because it's _____. It's only 150 words, and I told you to
   (short)
   write at least 250 words.

9. A: Can I borrow your bike?

   B: No, there's something wrong with the brakes. It's _____ to ride.
   (safe)

10. A: Dad, can we go in the water now?

   B: I don't know. It was cold before. Put your toe in the water and see if it's

   _____ now.
   (warm)

11. A: Why aren't the plants in the living room growing?

   B: Probably because it's _____. They need more light.
   (sunny)

7 **AS + ADJECTIVE + AS, *THE SAME* (+ NOUN) *AS, DIFFERENT FROM***

Put a check (✓) next to the sentences that are true.

_____ **1.** Canada is the same size as the United States.

_____ **2.** Lions are not as big as elephants.

_____ **3.** 32° F is the same temperature as 0° C.

_____ **4.** The Statue of Liberty in New York is not as old as the Pyramids in Egypt.

_____ **5.** Alaska is as cold as Antarctica.

_____ **6.** A whale is different from a fish.

_____ **7.** An orange is the same color as a carrot.

_____ **8.** Silver is as valuable as gold.

8 **THAN VS. AS**

Complete the sentences. Use **as** *or* **than***.*

1. Russia is bigger _____*than*_____ the United States.

2. Is your classroom the same size _____*as*_____ the other classrooms?

3. South America is not as big _____ Asia.

4. English is more difficult _____ my native language.

5. The president of the United States is not the same age _____ the leader of my country.

6. I'm more tired today _____ I was yesterday.

7. Are doctors as rich _____ lawyers?

8. Are you as thin _____ your best friend?

(continued on next page)

9. Thelma's the same height _____ her brother.

10. Are animals more intelligent _____ human beings?

11. This book is better _____ that one.

12. Some people are friendlier _____ others.

❾ AS + ADJECTIVE + AS VS. MORE + ADJECTIVE + THAN

Write sentences. Use the adjective in parentheses and **as . . . as**, **not as . . . as**, *or* **more . . . than**. *(Remember:* **=** *means* **equals**, **<** *means* **less than;** **>** *means* **more than**.*)*

1. a Fiat < a Mercedes (expensive)

   A Fiat isn't as expensive as a Mercedes.

2. the book > the film (interesting)

   The book is more interesting than the film.

3. my apartment = your apartment (big)

   My apartment is as big as your apartment.

4. trains < airplanes (fast)

5. January = February (cold)

6. the chair = the sofa (comfortable)

7. the governor of Oregon < the president of the United States (famous)

8. the bank < the post office (far)

9. limes = lemons (sour)

10. jazz > rock music (relaxing)

11. chocolate ice cream < vanilla ice cream (good)

_____

12. some people > other people (violent)

_____

13. college < high school (easy)

_____

14. these boxes = those boxes (heavy)

_____

10 THE SAME + NOUN + AS

Write questions. Use **the same . . . as** *and a noun in the box.*

| age distance color height length price size weight |

1. _Is your sister's hair the same color as your hair?_____

No. My sister's hair is brown. My hair's black.

2. _____

No. I'm 1.69 meters tall. My brother's 1.78 meters tall.

3. _____

No. My mother's fifty-nine years old. My father's sixty-two.

4. _____

No. The dining room's smaller than the living room.

5. _____

Yes. The apples and the oranges are both sixty cents a pound.

6. _____

No. I'm thinner than my brother.

7. _____

No. *War and Peace* is much longer than *Crime and Punishment.*

8. _____

No. The subway station is farther than the bus stop.

⓫ THE SAME AS AND DIFFERENT FROM

Write sentences. Use **the same as** *or* **different from**.

1. a wife and a housewife

  A wife is different from a housewife.

2. the U.S.A. and the United States

  The U.S.A. is the same as the United States.

3. a bike and a bicycle

4. a TV and a television

5. North America and the United States

6. 10,362 and 10.362

7. 3×16 and 16×3

8. $16 \div 3$ and $3 \div 16$

9. $1 and £1

10. a snack bar and a restaurant

11. 12:00 P.M. and noon

12. a plane and an airplane

THE PAST PROGRESSIVE

❶ AFFIRMATIVE AND NEGATIVE STATEMENTS WITH THE PAST PROGRESSIVE

Put a check (✓) next to the sentences that are true.

_____ **1.** I was sleeping at six o'clock yesterday morning.

_____ **2.** While I was having dinner last night, the telephone rang.

_____ **3.** A year ago I was not studying English.

_____ **4.** Last week I saw a friend when I was walking down the street.

_____ **5.** My classmates and I were not taking a test at this time last week.

_____ **6.** While I was getting dressed yesterday, birds were singing outside my window.

_____ **7.** My family and I were watching TV at 9:30 last night.

_____ **8.** While I was doing my homework yesterday, I made some mistakes.

❷ AFFIRMATIVE STATEMENTS WITH THE PAST PROGRESSIVE

What were these people doing? Make guesses and write sentences. Use the words in the box and the past progressive.

buy some groceries	go to school	talk on the phone	~~wait for the bus~~
cook dinner	study	type	wait for a table
get gas	take a shower		

1. I saw Lulu and Bertha at the bus stop.

    They were waiting for the bus.

2. I called Lulu yesterday, but her line was busy.

3. I saw Uncle Bob and Aunt Valerie at the Hillside Restaurant.

193

(continued on next page)

4. I saw Carol and Yoko at the library last night.

_____

5. I saw Pete's new secretary in the office.

_____

6. I saw Pete at the supermarket.

_____

7. When I called Elenore, she was in the bathroom.

_____

8. When I arrived at Norma's apartment, she was in the kitchen.

_____

9. When I went to the gas station, Milt was there.

_____

10. I saw Doug on 82nd Street.

_____

3 AFFIRMATIVE AND NEGATIVE STATEMENTS WITH THE PAST PROGRESSIVE

Write affirmative or negative sentences about the picture on page 47.
Use the past progressive.

1. When I saw Doug at the fruit store, he _____was standing_____ in line.
   (stand)

2. When I saw Doug at the fruit store, he _____wasn't eating_____ an apple.
   (eat)

3. When I saw Doug at the fruit store, he _____.
   (read)

4. When I saw Doug at the fruit store, three other people _____
   in line.   (wait)

5. When I saw Doug at the fruit store, the other people _____
   in front of him.   (stand)

6. When I saw Doug at the fruit store, he _____ pants.
   (wear)

7. When I saw Doug at the fruit store, he _____ his
   history book.   (hold)

8. When I saw Doug at the fruit store, he (buy) _____ bananas.
(buy)

9. When I saw Doug at the fruit store, the other customers _____.
(leave)

---

4 **THE SIMPLE PAST AND THE PAST PROGRESSIVE**

Write sentences. Use the past progressive and the simple past in each sentence.

1. When / the teacher / ask / me a question / I / read

　　 When the teacher asked me a question, I was reading.

2. While / my father / talk / to me / someone / ring / the doorbell

_____

3. The boys / play / basketball / when / the fight / start

_____

4. I / swim / when / I / get / a pain in my leg

_____

5. When / we / see / the accident / we / drive / down Market Street

_____

6. The doctor / examine / Mrs. May / when / she / scream

_____

7. While / I / wash / my hair / I / get / some soap in my eyes

_____

8. Alan / shave / when / he / cut / himself

_____

9. The train / come / while / we / get / our tickets

_____

5 YES / NO QUESTIONS WITH THE PAST PROGRESSIVE

Write questions. Use the past progressive.

1. **A:** Simon and Barbara have breakfast between 7:00 and 7:30 every morning.

   B: ___Were they having breakfast___ yesterday morning at 7:15?

   A: I think so.

2. **A:** Simon meets with his salespeople every morning between 9:00 and 9:30.

   B: _____ at 9:20 yesterday morning?

   A: Probably.

3. **A:** Barbara teaches every day between one o'clock and four o'clock.

   B: _____ yesterday at three o'clock?

   A: Of course.

4. **A:** Simon swims every Monday and Wednesday between noon and 12:45.

   B: _____ last Wednesday at 12:30?

   A: Probably.

5. **A:** Barbara practices the piano every morning between 9:00 and 10:00.

   B: _____ at 9:30 yesterday morning?

   A: Almost definitely.

6. **A:** Simon listens to a business report on the radio every afternoon between 4:30 and 5:00.

   B: _____ at 4:45 yesterday afternoon?

   A: I guess so.

7. **A:** Simon and Barbara have dinner between six o'clock and seven o'clock.

   B: _____ at 6:30 yesterday?

   A: Yes.

8. A: Simon and Barbara watch the news every evening between 7:00 and 7:30.

   B: _____ yesterday evening at 7:15?

   A: I think so.

9. A: Barbara takes a bath every evening between 9:00 and 9:30.

   B: _____ at 9:15 yesterday evening?

   A: Probably.

---

6 **THE SIMPLE PAST VS. THE PAST PROGRESSIVE**

Answer the questions. Use the simple past or the past progressive of the verbs in parentheses.

1a. A: What were you doing when it started to rain?

   B: We _____ *were having* _____ a picnic.
                      (have)

1b. A: What did you do when it started to rain?

   B: We _____ to the car.
                      (hurry)

2a. A: What were you doing when the phone rang?

   B: I _____ TV.
                      (watch)

2b. A: What did you do when the phone rang?

   B: I _____ it.
                      (answer)

3a. A: What were the children doing when the fire started?

   B: They _____ .
                      (sleep)

3b. A: What did the children do when the fire started?

   B: They _____ out of the house.
                      (run)

4a. A: What were you doing when the teacher came in?

   B: We _____ around.
                      (stand)

4b. A: What did you do when the teacher came in?

   B: We _____ down.
                      (sit)

(continued on next page)

5a. A: What was Susan doing when she fell?

B: She _____ a tree.
(climb)

5b. A: What did Susan do when she fell?

B: She _____ her mother.
(call)

6a. A: What was your father doing when he burned his hand?

B: He _____ .
(iron)

6b. A: What did your father do when he burned his hand?

B: He _____ some ice on the burn.
(put)

7 WH- QUESTIONS WITH THE PAST PROGRESSIVE

Write questions. Use **who, what, when, where, why,** *or* **how fast** *and the verbs in the box.*

| do   drive   go   ride   ~~stand~~   wait |

1. A: ___Where were you standing___ when the accident happened?

B: I was standing on the corner of Buick and 3rd Street.

2. A: _____?

B: I was waiting.

3. A: _____?

B: I was waiting for the bus.

4. A: _____?

B: I was going to the gym.

5. A: _____?

B: Because I always go to the gym on Mondays.

6. A: _____ the red car?

   B: A teenager was driving it.

7. A: _____?

B: He was going at least 65 miles per hour.

8. A: _____?

B: I don't know. Maybe he was driving so fast because the passenger was ill.

9. A: _____ in the car with him?

   B: An older woman. Maybe it was his mother.

UNIT

42 SHOULD, SHOULDN'T, OUGHT TO, HAD BETTER, AND HAD BETTER NOT

❶ AFFIRMATIVE AND NEGATIVE STATEMENTS WITH SHOULD

Complete the sentences. Use **should** *or* **shouldn't**.

1. Children ____shouldn't____ play with matches.

2. Children _____ watch television all day long.

3. Children _____ listen to their parents.

4. Children _____ eat a lot of candy.

5. Children _____ play in the street.

6. Teenagers _____ pay attention in school.

7. Teenagers _____ keep their bedrooms neat.

8. Teenagers _____ stay out all night with their friends.

9. Adults _____ exercise at least twice a week.

10. Adults _____ drink ten cups of coffee a day.

❷ AFFIRMATIVE STATEMENTS WITH OUGHT TO

Rewrite the sentences. Use **ought to**.

1. You should go to the dentist twice a year.

    You ought to go to the dentist twice a year.

2. I should visit my grandparents more often.

    _____

3. All passengers should arrive at the airport an hour before their flights.

    _____

4. Carol should study harder.

_____

5. We should take something to the party.

_____

❸ AFFIRMATIVE STATEMENTS WITH *SHOULD*

Rewrite the sentences. Use **should**.

1. Carol ought to clean her room more often.

  _Carol should clean her room more often._____

2. You ought to cook the meat a little longer.

_____

3. Lulu ought to be nicer to Elenore.

_____

4. I ought to learn how to type.

_____

5. Pete and Elenore ought to move into a smaller apartment.

_____

❹ AFFIRMATIVE AND NEGATIVE STATEMENTS WITH *SHOULD*

Complete the sentences. Use **should** *or* **shouldn't** *and the words in the box.*

~~see a doctor~~	leave early	study more	wash it
go to the dentist	look for another one	touch it	watch it
leave a tip	smoke		

1. Dave is sick. He _should see a doctor._____

2. I don't like my job. I _____

3. John often has a bad cough. He _____

(continued on next page)

4. Myra has a toothache. She _____

5. The car is dirty. We _____

6. The waiter is terrible. We _____

7. Doug and Jason aren't doing well in math. They _____

8. There's going to be a lot of traffic. We _____

9. That movie is very violent. The children _____

10. That dog may bite. You _____

5 WH- QUESTIONS WITH *SHOULD*

Complete the conversation. Write questions with **should***. Use* **who,**
what, when, where, why, *or* **how many** *and the verbs in parentheses.*

A: Let's have a party.

B: Okay. _____ When should we have _____ it?
                        1. (have)

A: Let's have it on March 23rd.

B: _____ it then?
                2. (have)

A: Because it's Lucy's birthday.

B: Oh, that's right. _____?
                        3. (invite)

A: Probably around twenty-five people.

B: _____?
        4. (invite)

A: Let's see . . . the neighbors, Lucy's family, the people from the office.

B: _____?
        5. (buy)

A: Well, we'll need drinks, potato chips, and things like that.

B: _____?
        6. (cook)

A: I'll make some lasagna.

B: That sounds good. I'll make some salad. _____ a
       birthday cake?   **7. (get)**

A: I like the Savoy Bakery's cakes.

B: Okay. Let's order one from there.

A: You know, we don't have enough dishes and glasses for twenty-five people.

_____?

8. (do)

B: That's no problem. We can get paper plates and cups at the supermarket.

A: You're right. That's a good idea. _____ out the invitations?

9. (send)

B: I'll write them this weekend.

6 AFFIRMATIVE AND NEGATIVE STATEMENTS WITH *HAD BETTER*

Match the situations with the advice.

__c__ **1.** We'd better take a taxi.

_____ **2.** We'd better ask for directions.

_____ **3.** We'd better not stay up late.

_____ **4.** We'd better make sure everything is locked.

_____ **5.** We'd better look at a map.

_____ **6.** We'd better not wait for the bus.

_____ **7.** We'd better not stay in the sun anymore.

_____ **8.** We'd better get a good night's sleep.

_____ **9.** We'd better throw away the food in the refrigerator.

_____ **10.** We'd better put some cream on our arms and legs.

a. We're lost.

b. We're getting red.

c. We're going to be late.

d. We'll be away for three weeks.

e. We have an exam tomorrow.

7 AFFIRMATIVE AND NEGATIVE STATEMENTS WITH *HAD BETTER*

Don and Amy are planning a dinner party. Complete the conversation.
Use **had better** *or* **had better not** *and the words in the box.*

ask Costas to bring her	invite him	rent a video
borrow some from the neighbors	let the dog in the house	serve shrimp
get a couple of bottles	~~make roast beef~~	sit together at the table

DON: What kind of food should we make? How about roast beef?

AMY: Alan can't eat beef.

DON: Well, then we _____ had better not make roast beef _____. How about shrimp?
                                             1.

AMY: Joan doesn't like fish or seafood.

DON: Then we _____. How about chicken?
                          2.

AMY: Good idea. Do we have enough drinks?

DON: Ed drinks only Diet Coke. We _____. Is Chris
                                                  3.
coming? She's allergic to animals. We _____.
                                                  4.

AMY: How is Sandy getting here? She doesn't drive and lives far from here.

DON: We _____.
                  5.

AMY: What do you think of the seating plan?

DON: Marsha and Sophia _____. They don't like each
                                        6.
other.

AMY: I just remembered Tonya has a new boyfriend. We

_____. And Ted and Marsha are bringing their
            7.
children.

DON: They will probably get bored. We _____.
                                                      8.

AMY: How many guests are coming? We won't have enough chairs.

DON: We _____.
                  9.

HAVE TO, DON'T HAVE TO, MUST, MUSTN'T

1 PRESENT AND PAST AFFIRMATIVE AND NEGATIVE STATEMENTS WITH *HAVE TO*

Put a check (✓) next to the sentences that are true.

_____ **1.** People in my country have to pay taxes.

_____ **2.** People in my country don't have to vote.

_____ **3.** Drivers in my country have to have driver's licenses.

_____ **4.** Students in my country don't have to wear uniforms in high school.

_____ **5.** Young people in my country don't have to do military service.

_____ **6.** Women in my country had to obey their husbands fifty years ago.

_____ **7.** Children in my country did not have to go to school fifty years ago.

_____ **8.** Children in my country had to go to work at a young age fifty years ago.

2 AFFIRMATIVE AND NEGATIVE STATEMENTS WITH *HAVE TO*

Complete the sentences. Use **have to** *and* **don't have to** *in each sentence.*

1. Students ___don't have to___ stay in school twelve hours a day, but they ___have to___ study.

2. Teachers _____ correct papers, but they _____ wear uniforms.

3. Police officers _____ speak a foreign language, but they _____ wear uniforms.

4. Doctors _____ study for many years, but they _____ know how to type.

205

(continued on next page)

5. Secretaries _____ work at night, but they _____ know how to type.

6. Firefighters _____ work at night, but they _____ study for many years.

7. Fashion models _____ work seven days a week, but they _____ worry about their appearance.

8. Farmers _____ get up early in the morning, but they _____ worry about their appearance.

9. Basketball players _____ practice regularly, but they _____ play a game every day.

10. Accountants _____ be good writers, but they _____ be good with numbers.

3 **AFFIRMATIVE AND NEGATIVE STATEMENTS WITH *HAVE TO***

Complete the conversations. Use **have to**, **has to**, **don't have to**, *or* **doesn't have to**.

1. **A:** Is Dan getting up early this morning?

   B: No, he _doesn't have to get up early this morning_. There's no school.

2. **A:** Is Sheila leaving early today?

   B: Yes, she _____. She has an appointment with her dentist.

3. **A:** Are you going food shopping today?

   B: Yes, I _____. There's no food in the house.

4. **A:** Are you and your wife coming by taxi?

   B: Yes, we _____. Our car isn't working.

5. **A:** Is Barbara working late today?

   B: No, she _____. Her boss is on vacation.

6. **A:** Are the children cleaning up their room?

   B: No, they _____. I cleaned it up yesterday.

7. A: Is Mary taking some medicine?

   B: Yes, she _____. She has a stomach problem.

8. A: Are you paying for the tickets?

   B: No, we _____. They're free.

9. A: Is José wearing a suit and tie this morning?

   B: Yes, he _____. He has an important business

   meeting.

10. A: Does Bonnie do housework?

   B: No, she _____. She has a maid.

---

④ PRESENT AND PAST AFFIRMATIVE AND NEGATIVE STATEMENTS WITH *HAVE TO*

Rewrite the sentences. Use **have to**, **has to**, **don't have to**, **doesn't have to**, **had to**, *or* **didn't have to**.

1. It's necessary for me to finish this exercise.

   I   *have to finish this exercise.* _____

2. It isn't necessary for me to do the last exercise again.

   I _____

3. It wasn't necessary for Doug to go to school yesterday.

   Doug _____

4. It was necessary for Carol to clean her room yesterday.

   Carol _____

5. It isn't necessary for Yoko to write her parents every week.

   Yoko _____

6. It wasn't necessary for Pete and Elenore to go shopping last week.

   Pete and Elenore _____

7. It's necessary for my classmates and me to take tests.

   My classmates and I _____

8. It isn't necessary for Pete and Elenore to buy a new car.

   Pete and Elenore _____

(continued on next page)

9. It's necessary for Lulu to see her doctor today.

Lulu _____

10. It's necessary for me to check my answers to this exercise.

I _____

5 **AFFIRMATIVE AND NEGATIVE STATEMENTS WITH *MUST***

What does each sign mean? Write sentences. Use **must** *or* **mustn't** *and the words in the box.*

drive faster than 55 mph	make a U-turn	stop
~~enter~~	park in this area	turn left
go more slowly	pass	turn right

1. DO NOT ENTER

2. STOP

3. (no right turn sign)

4. (no left turn sign)

5. SPEED LIMIT 55

6. NO PARKING ANY TIME

7. (no U-turn sign)

8. (no passing sign)

9. MEN AT WORK

1. You mustn't enter. _____

2. _____

3. _____

4. _____

5. _____

6. _____

7. _____

8. _____

9. _____

6 AFFIRMATIVE AND NEGATIVE STATEMENTS WITH *HAD TO*

Mr. and Mrs. Chung were on vacation last week. Write sentences. Use
had to *or* **didn't have to**.

~~do anything special~~	look for a hotel
find someone to take care of their dog	make the bed every morning
get to the airport on time	pack and unpack suitcases
get up early every morning	pay their hotel bill
go to work	wash dishes

1. ___They didn't have to do anything special._____

2. _____

3. _____

4. _____

5. _____

6. _____

7. _____

8. _____

9. _____

10. _____

7 PAST AND PRESENT *YES / NO* QUESTIONS AND SHORT ANSWERS WITH *HAVE TO*

*Write questions. Use **have to**. Then answer the questions. Use short answers.*

1. have / English / in class / you / to / do / speak

   Do you have to speak English in class?

   Yes, we do. (OR: No, we don't.)

2. get up / to / your / have / does / in the morning / at 6:00 / mother

   _____

   _____

3. you / to / last night / cook / did / have

   _____

   _____

4. best friend / do / does / to / have / your / this exercise

   _____

   _____

5. to / you / on time / in / have / English class / do / be

   _____

   _____

6. friends / learn / to / do / English / your / have

   _____

   _____

7. shave / father / have / your / did / to / yesterday

   _____

   _____

8. your / to work / to / best friend / yesterday / did / have / go

   _____

   _____

9. a / to / test / you / have / did / last week / take

   _____

   _____

8 PAST AND PRESENT *WH-* QUESTIONS WITH *HAVE TO*

Write questions. Use **have to**.

1. I have to buy some food.

   What _do you have to buy?_____

2. She has to get a book from the library.

   Why _____

3. He has to go.

   Where _____

4. The teacher had to talk to someone.

   Who _____

5. We had to stay there a long time.

   How long _____

6. The students have to stay after class.

   Why _____

7. I have to use eggs.

   How many eggs _____

8. The high school students had to send their college applications.

   When _____

9. I have to get up early.

   What time _____

10. He had to borrow some money.

    How much money _____

SUPERLATIVE FORM OF ADJECTIVES AND ADVERBS

❶ THE SUPERLATIVE FORM OF ADJECTIVES AND ADVERBS

Answer the questions about the Winston family. Write **Carol**, **Doug**, *or* **Norma**. *(Look at your Student Book if you need help.)*

1. Who's the oldest? _____Norma_____

2. Who's the youngest? _____

3. Who's the neatest? _____

4. Who lives the farthest from home? _____

5. Who's the most serious of the three? _____

6. Who has the busiest social life? _____

❷ THE SUPERLATIVE FORM OF ADJECTIVES

Complete the sentences. Use the superlative form of the adjective.

1. The kitchen is always hot. It's _____the hottest_____ room in the house.

2. Roger's a bad student. He's _____ student in the class.

3. Chemistry is hard. For me, it's _____ subject in school.

4. Roses are beautiful. In fact, many people think that roses are _____ flowers.

5. Noon is a busy time at the bank. In fact, it's _____ time.

6. "Married Young" is a funny program. It's _____ program on TV.

7. Scully's is a good restaurant. In fact, it's _____ restaurant in town.

8. I think monkeys are ugly. In my opinion, they're _____ animals in the zoo.

9. Midnight is a popular nightclub. It's _____ nightclub in town.

10. Dixon's has low prices. It has _____ prices in the neighborhood.

11. Pamela's a fast swimmer. She's _____ swimmer on the team.

12. Jake is charming. He's _____ of all my friends.

3 THE COMPARATIVE AND SUPERLATIVE FORM OF ADJECTIVES

Write two sentences. Use the superlative form of the adjective in parentheses for one sentence. Use the comparative form for the other.

1. a train / a plane / a bus (fast)

   a. _A plane is the fastest of the three._

   b. _A train is faster than a bus._

2. a teenager / a child / a baby (old)

   a. _____

   b. _____

3. a Ford / a Rolls Royce / a BMW (expensive)

   a. _____

   b. _____

4. Nigeria / Spain / Sweden (hot)

   a. _____

   b. _____

(continued on next page)

5. a street / a path / a highway (wide)

    a. _____

    b. _____

6. a city / a village / a town (big)

    a. _____

    b. _____

7. an elephant / a gorilla / a fox (heavy)

    a. _____

    b. _____

8. an hour / a second / a minute (long)

    a. _____

    b. _____

9. boxing / golf / soccer (dangerous)

    a. _____

    b. _____

10. a banana / a carrot / chocolate (fattening)

    a. _____

    b. _____

4 THE SUPERLATIVE FORM OF ADVERBS

Write sentences. Use the superlative form of the adverbs in parentheses.

1. Andy came at 6:00. Mike came at 6:20. Jean came at 6:40.

    a. (late)   _Jean came the latest._ _____

    b. (early) _____

2. The red car is going fifty miles per hour. The blue car is going sixty-five miles per hour. The white car's going seventy-three miles per hour.

    a. (slowly) _____

    b. (fast) _____

3. Shirley drives well and never has car accidents. Maurice usually drives well, but he had an accident last year. Fran drives badly. She had two accidents last year and one accident this year.

   a. (dangerously) _____

   b. (carefully) _____

4. Gary works two miles from his home. Viv works fifteen miles from her home. Harris works thirty miles from his home.

   a. (close) _____

   b. (far) _____

5. Milton speaks a few words of Spanish. Linda can speak Spanish, but she often makes mistakes. Carolyn speaks Spanish and never makes mistakes.

   a. (well) _____

   b. (badly) _____

6. Sam types fifty words a minute, but he always makes at least six mistakes. Joan types sixty words a minute, but she doesn't usually make any mistakes. Renée types seventy-five words a minute, but she often makes two or three mistakes.

   a. (quickly) _____

   b. (accurately) _____

PUTTING IT ALL TOGETHER

REVIEW OF VERB TENSES AND MODALS

① VERB TENSE REVIEW

Find the thirteen verb tense mistakes in the postcard. Then correct them.

> May 22nd
>
> Dear Mom and Dad,
>
>   Greetings from Venice. Dan and I ~~am~~ *are* fine. We have a wonderful time on our honeymoon. The weather isn't great, but Venice be such a romantic place. It have so many beautiful places.
>
>   Yesterday we walk all around the city. We visit several churches. They was so wonderful, and we see so many gorgeous paintings.
>
>   Today it rained all morning, so we didn't went far from our hotel. This afternoon we have lunch at a very good restaurant across from the hotel. We both eat special Venetian dishes and enjoyed them very much.
>
>   It is five o'clock now, and Dan rests. Tonight after dinner we take a gondola ride. I can't wait!
>
>   Love,
>
>   Carol

② VERB TENSE REVIEW AND *WH-* QUESTIONS

Read Carol's diary. Then write questions. Use **who, what, when,
where, what time, how long,** *or* **why.**

May 20th

 Venice is such a wonderful place. We arrived at eleven o'clock this
morning, and I already love it. I still can't believe it, but we took a boat
from the airport to our hotel on the Grand Canal. Tonight we're going to
take a gondola ride.

---

1. When did they arrive in Venice?

At eleven o'clock on May 20th.

2. _____

It's on the Grand Canal.

3. _____

They're going to take a gondola ride.

May 21st

 Well, it rained all night last night, so we stayed in our hotel. I really
wanted to go on the gondola ride, but it was impossible in the rain.

 Today we're going on a walking tour of the city. The tour will start at
9:00. (It's 7:30 now, and Dan is sleeping.) The tour guide is a
professor of art history at the university here. I think it will be interesting.

 In the evening we're going to have dinner at a restaurant near Piazza
San Marco with two people from Canada. We met them yesterday on the
boat ride from the airport. Their names are Paul and Myra, and they're
going to stay in Venice for two weeks.

(continued on next page)

4. _____

Because it rained all night.

5. _____

On a walking tour of the city.

6. _____

At 9:00.

7. _____

He's sleeping.

8. _____

A professor of art history.

9. _____

At a restaurant near Piazza San Marco.

10. _____

With two people from Canada.

11. _____

Yesterday.

12. _____

Paul and Myra.

13. _____

For two weeks.

May 22nd
Dinner was great. Paul is a little strange, but I like Myra a lot. Paul
and Dan ate too much. Dan was sick all night and didn't fall asleep
until five in the morning. It's already 8:30, and he's still sleeping.
Dan loves to sleep. (I didn't know that before the wedding. It's okay.
I love him anyway!)

14. _____

Myra.

15. _____

He ate too much.

16. _____

He loves to sleep.

---

③ REVIEW OF MODALS

How will Carol and Dan's life change after marriage? Complete the sentences. Circle the best answers and write them on the lines.

1. Carol and Dan _____have to_____ find a place to live.

   a. may

   ⓑ have to

2. Dan _____ go out with other women.

   a. mustn't

   b. doesn't have to

3. Carol and Dan _____ buy a house.

   a. may

   b. must

4. Carol and Dan _____ have a lot of children.

   a. might

   b. have to

5. Carol _____ fight a lot with Dan.

   a. can't

   b. shouldn't

6. Carol and Dan _____ be honest with each other.

   a. can

   b. should

(continued on next page)

7. Carol and Dan _____ earn money.

   a. may

   b. have to

8. Carol's parents _____ say bad things about Dan.

   a. don't have to

   b. shouldn't

9. Carol and Dan _____ help each other with problems.

   a. ought to

   b. mustn't

10. Carol and Dan _____ listen to Carol's parents.

   a. can't

   b. don't have to

11. Carol _____ be rude to Dan's family.

   a. mustn't

   b. doesn't have to

REVIEW OF VERB TENSES AND COMPARISONS

 COMPARATIVE FORM OF ADJECTIVES AND ADVERBS

Yoko had Teacher A this year and Teacher B last year. She liked Teacher A more. Here are the reasons. Compare the two teachers. Write sentences.

Teacher A	Teacher B
1. Teacher A is very patient.	Teacher B isn't very patient.
2. Teacher A is organized.	Teacher B isn't organized.
3. Teacher A is nice.	Teacher B isn't very nice.
4. Teacher A teaches well.	Teacher B doesn't teach well.
5. Teacher A speaks clearly.	Teacher B doesn't speak clearly.
6. Teacher A is friendly.	Teacher B isn't very friendly.
7. Teacher A gives back homework quickly.	Teacher B doesn't give back homework quickly.
8. Teacher A explains things slowly.	Teacher B doesn't explain things slowly.
9. The atmosphere in Teacher A's class is relaxed.	The atmosphere in Teacher B's class isn't relaxed.
10. The homework in Teacher A's class is easy.	The homework in Teacher B's class is difficult.
11. The books in Teacher A's class are interesting.	The books in Teacher B's class aren't very interesting.
12. Unfortunately, the tests in Teacher A's class are hard.	The tests in Teacher B's class aren't hard.

1. ___Teacher A is more patient than Teacher B.___

2. _____

3. _____

4. _____

5. _____

6. _____

7. _____

8. _____

9. _____

10. _____

11. _____

12. _____

2 SENTENCES WITH *NOT AS . . . AS*

Rewrite the sentences in Exercise 4. Use **not as . . . as**.

1. Teacher B isn't as patient as Teacher A.

2. _____

3. _____

4. _____

5. _____

6. _____

7. _____

8. _____

9. _____

10. _____

11. _____

12. _____

REVIEW OF VERB TENSES, NOUNS, AND QUANTIFIERS

1 QUANTIFIERS AND COUNT AND NON-COUNT NOUNS

Find the ten differences between the pictures. Write sentences. Use **a few**, **a little**, *or* **a lot of**.

1. There are a few dishes in the first picture, but there are a lot of
    dishes in the second picture.

2. _____

    _____

3. _____

    _____

(continued on next page)

4. _____

_____

5. _____

_____

6. _____

_____

7. _____

_____

8. _____

_____

9. _____

_____

10. _____

_____

② YES / NO QUESTIONS WITH *MANY* AND *MUCH*

Write questions about the first picture on page 223. Use **many** *or* **much** *and the words in the box. Then answer the questions.*

~~dishes~~	chairs	flowers	glasses
bread	cheese	fruit	orange juice
butter	chocolate	gifts	potato chips

1. ___Are there many dishes?_____

___No, there aren't._____

2. _____

_____

3. _____

_____

4. _____

_____

5. _____

_____

6. _____

_____

7. _____

_____

8. _____

_____

9. _____

_____

10. _____

_____

11. _____

_____

12. _____

_____

ANSWER KEY

Where the full form is given, the contraction is also acceptable. Where the contracted form is given, the full form is also acceptable, unless the exercise is about contractions.

PART VII REVIEW OF THE SIMPLE PRESENT TENSE AND THE PRESENT PROGRESSIVE

UNIT PRESENT AND PRESENT PROGRESSIVE; *HOW OFTEN . . . ?*; ADVERBS AND EXPRESSIONS OF FREQUENCY

 1

3, 4, 7, 8, and 9 are true.

2

3. I rarely practice in the middle of the night.
4. I seldom fight with customers.
5. I often drive at night.
6. I am always careful.
7. I almost always find the problem with the car.
8. I never put lemon in milk.
9. I am bored once in a while.
10. The hospital is open every day.
11. I almost never wear a suit and tie to work.
12. We are frequently away from home for three OR four days at a time.

3

2. How often does Donna play basketball? She frequently plays basketball.
3. How often does David swim? He never swims.

4. How often do Barbara and Ed play basketball? They never play basketball.
5. How often does Ed jog? He often jogs.
6. How often does Barbara swim? She swims three times a week.
7. How often do Barbara and David jog? They rarely jog.
8. How often do Ed and George swim? They swim once or twice a week.
9. How often do George and David play basketball? They play basketball almost every day.
10. How often does George jog? He almost never jogs.
11. How often do you jog?
12. How often do you do exercises?

4

2. a	5. c	8. h	11. j
3. b	6. f	9. l	12. g
4. e	7. k	10. d	

5

2. drives, is (OR 's) driving a bus
3. fixes cars, is (OR 's) fixing cars
4. serves food, is (OR 's) serving food
5. paint pictures, are (OR 're) painting pictures
6. do experiments, (OR 're) doing experiments
7. write articles, are (OR 're) writing articles
8. cuts meat, is (OR 's) cutting meat
9. counts money, is (OR 's) counting money
10. bake bread and cake, are (OR 're) baking bread and cake

AK1

11. waters plants and flowers, is (OR 's) watering plants and flowers
12. feeds animals, is (OR 's) feeding animals

6

2. Are you doing
3. am cutting
4. Do you prepare
5. eat
6. do you have
7. eat
8. go
9. are getting
10. doesn't go
11. Do your kids go
12. don't stay up
13. get up

14. are
15. does your daughter do
16. Does she watch
17. practices
18. is practicing
19. does she practice
20. Does she play
21. are
22. am working
23. is
24. Do you have

UNIT NON-ACTION VERBS

1

3. have, non-action verb
4. is having, action verb
5. belongs, non-action verb
6. need, non-action verb
7. like, non-action verb
8. come, action verb
9. smell, non-action verb
10. are . . . smelling, action verb
11. do, action verb
12. hate, non-action verb
13. know, non-action verb
14. are running, action verb

2

2. a	6. b	10. a	14. a
3. b	7. a	11. a	
4. a	8. b	12. b	
5. a	9. a	13. b	

3

2. don't care
3. Do you want
4. is playing
5. don't know
6. don't have
7. is raining
8. have
9. don't have
10. don't need
11. like
12. wants

13. don't think
14. has
15. is doing
16. hear
17. is talking
18. is talking
19. doesn't understand
20. is getting
21. do you know
22. know
23. don't know

UNIT VERBS PLUS NOUNS, GERUNDS, AND INFINITIVES

1

2. i	4. a	6. e	8. g
3. b	5. c	7. h	9. f

2

2. Milt is good at fixing things.
3. Pete enjoys fishing.
4. Elenore is interested in collecting stamps.
5. Norma enjoys gardening.
6. Carol is good at riding horses.
7. Lulu is interested in learning Spanish.
8. Yoko is good at cooking.

3

2. to swim (OR swimming)
3. to help
4. to talk
5. to move
6. to be
7. to receive (OR receiving)
8. to study (OR studying)
9. to relax
10. studying

UNIT POSSESSIVE ADJECTIVES AND POSSESSIVE PRONOUNS

1

3. correct
4. correct
5. Please bring me my car.
6. Where is her car?
7. correct
8. correct
9. We need our car.
10. Their car is expensive.
11. correct
12. Why do you want your car?

2

2. Mine		5. Yours		8. hers	
3. his		6. theirs		9. Theirs	
4. ours		7. his		10. ours	

3

2. my, yours, mine
3. hers, hers
4. our, ours
5. Their, their, theirs
6. his, his

PART VIII **REVIEW OF THE SIMPLE PAST TENSE; NEGATIVE QUESTIONS; THE FUTURE**

UNIT 29 **REVIEW OF THE SIMPLE PAST TENSE; NEGATIVE QUESTIONS**

1

2. made
3. left
4. were
5. didn't have
6. didn't play
7. bought
8. didn't eat
9. watched

2

2. No, they weren't. (OR Yes, they were.)
3. Yes, I did. (OR No, I didn't.)
4. Yes, he was. (OR No, he wasn't.)
5. Yes, it was. (OR No, it wasn't.)
6. Yes, I did. (OR No, I didn't.)
7. Yes, I was. (OR No, I wasn't.)
8. No, they didn't. (OR Yes, they did.)
9. Yes, we did. (OR No, we didn't.)
10. Yes, it was. (OR No, it wasn't.)
11. Yes, he / she did. (OR No, he / she didn't.)
12. Yes, I was. (OR No, I wasn't.)

3

2. Were they on sale? Yes, they were only $25.
3. Were you at home last night? No, I was at the library.
4. Were the guests late for the party? No, they were all on time.
5. Was it warm in Australia? The weather was beautiful every day.
6. Was the movie good? It was okay.
7. Were the people at the party friendly? Most of them were very nice.
8. Was he there? No, he was at a meeting.

4

2. Didn't you eat
3. Weren't you
4. Didn't it rain
5. Didn't you like
6. Wasn't
7. Didn't you see

UNIT 30 **WH- QUESTIONS IN THE SIMPLE PAST TENSE**

1

2. b
3. a
4. b
5. a
6. a
7. b
8. b
9. b
10. a

2

2. f, were
3. i, did
4. b, was
5. a, were
6. c, did
7. j, was
8. l, did
9. d, was
10. k, was
11. g, did
12. h, were

3

2. were you
3. was it
4. were they afraid
5. was the score
6. was the name of the store
7. were they born
8. were they here
9. were you with (OR was with you)
10. was Eleanor Roosevelt

UNIT 31 **BE GOING TO FOR THE FUTURE; FUTURE AND PAST TIME MARKERS**

1

2. this evening
3. next month
4. tomorrow morning
5. next week
6. tonight
7. tomorrow night (OR this week)

2

2. in two weeks
3. in three days
4. in two months
5. in ten minutes

3

(Answers will vary.)

4

(Possible answers)
I am (OR am not) going to study.
I am (OR am not) going to go shopping.
I am (OR am not) going to clean.
I am (OR am not) going to watch TV.
I am (OR am not) going to go out with friends.
I am (OR am not) going to listen to music.
I am (OR am not) going to visit relatives.
I am (OR am not) going to talk on the telephone.
I am (OR am not) going to take a shower.
I am (OR am not) going to write a letter.
I am (OR am not) going to read a newspaper.
I am (OR am not) going to stay home.

5

(Possible answers)
2. She's going to study.
3. They're going to write letters.
4. They're going to ski.
5. He's going to listen to music.
6. He's going to take pictures.

6

2. She isn't going to take
3. She isn't going to take
4. They aren't going to play
5. They aren't going to watch
6. I'm not going to eat
7. We aren't going to swim
8. He isn't going to see
9. I'm not going to wake up
10. He isn't going to deliver

7

2. Who is going to cook tonight?
3. When is dinner going to be ready?
4. Why is he going to cook so much food?
5. How long is he going to need to cook the dinner?
6. Who is going to come?
7. How is he going to cook the lamb?
8. Where are all of your guests going to sit?
9. What are you going to do?
10. How long are your guests going to stay?

8

2. What is he going to make?
3. Why is he going to cook so much food?
4. How is he going to cook the lamb?
5. Who is going to come?
6. How long is he going to need to cook the dinner?
7. What are you going to do?
8. When is dinner going to be ready?
9. How long are your guests going to stay?
10. Where are all of your guests going to sit?

9

3. 'm doing, now
4. 're . . . going, future
5. 's leaving, future
6. Are . . . doing, now
7. Is . . . coming, future
8. are . . . listening, now
9. are . . . going, now
10. is . . . waiting, now

10

2. They are flying to London at 7:30 on May 8.
3. They are arriving in London at 6:45 A.M. on May 9.
4. They are staying at the London Regency Hotel on May 9 and 10.
5. They are visiting Buckingham Palace at 2 P.M. on May 9.
6. They are having tea at the Ritz Hotel at 4:30 on May 9.
7. They are going to the theater at 7:30 on May 9.
8. They are going on a tour of central London at 9:00 A.M. on May 10.
9. They are eating lunch at a typical English pub at twelve o'clock on May 10.
10. They are leaving for Scotland at 8:00 A.M. on May 11.

11

2. Are you going to the movies this weekend? Yes, I am. (OR No, I'm not.)
3. Are you taking a trip next week? Yes, I am. (OR No, I'm not.)
4. Can your friend leave in two hours? Yes, he / she can. (OR No, he / she can't.)
5. Are your classmates meeting you tonight? Yes, they are. (OR No, they aren't.)
6. Is your mother driving to work tomorrow? Yes, she is. (OR No, she isn't.)
7. Is your father taking an English class next year? Yes, he is. (OR No, he isn't.)
8. Are your neighbors doing anything this weekend? Yes, they are. (OR No, they aren't.)
9. Are you and your friends playing cards next Saturday? Yes, we are. (OR No, we aren't.)
10. Can your parents call your teacher tonight? Yes, they can. (OR No, they can't.)

12

2. When are you leaving?
3. How are you getting there? (OR How are you going?)
4. Why are you driving?
5. How long are you staying?
6. Who are you going with?
7. What are you taking?

UNIT *WILL* FOR THE FUTURE

2. I'll get you some water.
3. I'll help you.

4. I'll buy you some.
5. I'll turn on the air conditioner.
6. I'll make you a sandwich.
7. I'll get you some aspirin.
8. I'll drive you.
9. I'll wash them.

❷

2. He won't lose his job.
3. I'll have a cup of coffee.
4. It'll rain this evening.
5. She won't be happy.
6. They'll have a good time.
7. You won't like it.

❸

2.	a	4.	a	6.	b	8.	a
3.	b	5.	a	7.	b	9.	b

❹

2. I won't leave late.
3. It won't be hot.
4. Coffee won't cost more.
5. The dishes won't be dirty.
6. We won't come before seven o'clock.
7. Mr. and Mrs. McNamara won't buy a new car.
8. I won't make many eggs.
9. Valerie won't lose the game.
10. The parking lot won't be full.

❺

2. Will I be
3. will marry
4. will I meet
5. will be
6. Will she love
7. will we meet
8. won't have
9. will be
10. will I be
11. won't be
12. will bother
13. won't like
14. Will our home have
15. won't leave
16. won't bother
17. will become
18. Will that make

PART Ⅸ   NOUNS, ARTICLES, AND QUANTIFIERS; MODALS I

UNIT **COUNT AND NON-COUNT NOUNS AND QUANTIFIERS**

❶

2.	5	4.	1	6.	8	8.	1
3.	7	5.	9	7.	4	9.	8

10.	4	12.	7	14.	8
11.	5	13.	2	15.	3

❷

Count Nouns—eggs, vegetables, napkins, bags, potato chips, toothbrushes
Non-Count Nouns—ice cream, fruit, milk, rice, food, bread, fish

❸

Count Nouns—a student, some teeth, some children, some friends, an animal, some people, an uncle, a television, some questions, a computer
Non-Count Nouns—some water, some paper, some homework, some advice, some traffic, some furniture, some money, some information, some rain, some oil

❹

2.	a	5.	a	8.	b	11.	b
3.	a	6.	a	9.	a		
4.	b	7.	a	10.	a		

❺

2.	A	4.	the	6.	the, a	8.	a, a
3.	the	5.	a	7.	the, the		

❻

3. He bought some orange juice.
4. He didn't buy any lemons.
5. He bought a newspaper.
6. He didn't buy any bread.
7. He didn't buy any onions.
8. He didn't buy a toothbrush.
9. He bought some potatoes.
10. He didn't buy any lettuce.
11. He didn't buy any carrots.
12. He bought some butter.
13. He bought some milk.
14. He bought some eggs.

❼

(Answers will vary.)
a lot of / any—food in my refrigerator, money in my pocket, books next to my bed, shirts in my closet, friends, free time, children, work to do today, questions for my teacher, jewelry, medicine in my bathroom, problems with English grammar, photographs in my wallet, ice cream at home
a little / much—cheese in my pocket, food in my

refrigerator, money in my pocket, free time, work to do today, jewelry, medicine in my bathroom, ice cream at home

a few / many—books next to my bed, shirts in my closet, friends, children, questions for my teacher, problems with English grammar, photographs in my wallet

U N I T   34   QUESTIONS WITH *ANY* / *SOME* / *HOW MUCH* / *HOW MANY*; QUANTIFIERS; CONTAINERS

❶

2. d	**5.** g	**8.** e	**11.** j
3. a	**6.** h	**9.** l	**12.** i
4. c	**7.** f	**10.** k	

❷

3. One carton.	**6.** One.	**9.** One tube.
4. Two heads.	**7.** Four.	**10.** Two.
5. Three.	**8.** Three bars.	

❸

4. Is there any furniture in your home? Yes, there is. (OR No, there isn't.)
5. Are there any clothes in your closet? Yes, there are. (OR No, there aren't.)
6. Is there any money under your bed? Yes, there is. (OR No, there isn't.)
7. Is there an alarm clock next to your bed? Yes, there is. (OR No, there isn't.)
8. Is there any snow outside your home? Yes, there is. (OR No, there isn't.)
9. Is there a sink in your bathroom? Yes, there is. (OR No, there isn't.)
10. Are there any dishes in your kitchen sink? Yes, there are. (OR No, there aren't.)
11. Are there any pictures in your bedroom? Yes, there are. (OR No, there aren't.)
12. Is there any candy in your home? Yes, there is. (OR No, there isn't.)
13. Is there a window in your kitchen? Yes, there is. (OR No, there isn't.)
14. Is there a television in your living room? Yes, there is. (OR No, there isn't.)

❹

3. How much flour do you need?
4. How much sugar do you have?
5. How many bananas do you want?
6. How many oranges do you want?
7. How much cereal do you need?
8. How many potatoes do you need?
9. How much milk do you want?
10. How many roses do you want?
11. How many cookies do you have?
12. How much money do you have?

❺

2. There are too many days.
3. There are too many numbers.
4. There is too much water.
5. There is too much furniture.
6. There is too much food.
7. There are too many birds.
8. There is too much shampoo.
9. There are not enough batteries.
10. There is not enough toothpaste.
11. There is not enough air.
12. There are not enough chairs.

❻

3. There were too few people for two teams.
4. We had too little paper for everyone in the class.
5. There was too little food for fifteen people.
6. You have too little information.
7. There are too many bedrooms in that apartment.
8. We had too little time for that test.
9. There are too few bananas for a banana cake.
10. There are too few sales people at that store.

❼

2. b	**5.** a	**8.** a
3. a	**6.** b	**9.** b
4. b	**7.** b	**10.** a

U N I T   35   *CAN* AND *COULD* FOR ABILITY AND POSSIBILITY; *MAY I*, *CAN I*, AND *COULD I* FOR POLITE REQUESTS

❶

2. secretary	**4.** summer camp worker
3. driver	

❷

4. He can drive and lift 100 pounds.
5. He can type and speak Spanish.
6. She can play the guitar and draw.
7. He can't drive, and he can't lift 100 pounds.
8. She can type, but she can't speak Spanish.
9. She can lift 100 pounds, but she can't drive.
10. He can draw, but he can't play the guitar.
11. She can't draw, and she can't play the guitar.
12. He can't type, and he can't speak Spanish.

2. Can your mother lift 100 pounds? Yes, she can. (OR No, she can't.)
3. Can your father play the guitar? Yes, he can. (OR No, he can't.)
4. Can your best friend ride a horse? Yes, he / she can. (OR No, he / she can't.)
5. Can your parents speak Spanish? Yes, they can. (OR No, they can't.)
6. Can you swim? Yes, I can. (OR No, I can't.)
7. Can you type? Yes, I can. (OR No, I can't.)

2. could practice
3. couldn't go
4. couldn't understand
5. couldn't eat
6. could play
7. couldn't find
8. could hear
9. couldn't go
10. could do

2. Can I (OR May I) open the window?
3. Can I (OR May I) use the telephone?
4. Can I (OR May I) get a ride (with you)?
5. Can I (OR May I) use (OR borrow) your eraser?
6. Can I (OR May I) have a drink of water?
7. Can I (OR May I) ask you a question?
8. Can I (OR May I) sit at the empty table in the corner?

U N I T **36** *MAY* OR *MIGHT* FOR **POSSIBILITY**

3. permission
4. possibility
5. possibility
6. permission
7. possibility
8. permission
9. possibility
10. permission

2. We may (OR might) come by taxi.
3. He may (OR might) not want to come.
4. They may (OR might) study.
5. The store may (OR might) be closed.
6. She may (OR might) not finish the work by Friday.
7. The dog may (OR might) come home.
8. You may (OR might) not like that kind of food.
9. I may (OR might) not leave before seven o'clock.
10. The cookies may (OR might) not taste good.

3. may
4. will
5. will
6. may
7. may
8. will
9. will
10. may

3. may (OR might) have an accident.
4. may (OR might) break.
5. may (OR might) not win.
6. may (OR might) get lost.
7. may (OR might) not live.
8. may (OR might) bite.
9. may (OR might) get sick.
10. may (OR might) close.

U N I T **37** **DESIRES, INVITATIONS, REQUESTS:** *WOULD LIKE,* *WOULD YOU LIKE . . . ?,* *WOULD YOU PLEASE . . . ?*

1. At the bus station.
2. On an airplane.
3. At a movie theater.

3. Sheila would like to talk to you.
4. Would your parents like to come?
5. Sandy and Billy would like some coffee.
6. Would Dan like to come with us?
7. My friend and I would like a table for two.
8. Would the teacher like to come to the party?
9. I would like to take a long trip.
10. We would like you to have dinner with us.

2. Ari would like Conchita to bring the CDs.
3. Ari would like Irene and Amira to help with the cooking.
4. Ari would like Eric to bring his CD player.
5. Ari would like Harry, Mike, and Tom to move the furniture.
6. Ari would like Ellen to buy some ice cream.
7. Ari would like Victor to pick up the birthday cake.
8. Ari would like Carmen and Ted to keep Tony busy.
9. Ari would like Ratana to make the decorations.

2. Would you like
3. Would you like
4. would like

5. Would you like me to give
6. What would you like to do
7. Where would you like to go
8. Would you like to go
9. Would you like to see
10. What time would you like to go
11. would like to get
12. Where would you like to eat

5

2. Would (OR Could) you (please) give me the key to my room?
3. Would (OR Could) you (please) explain the meaning of the word *grateful*?
4. Would (OR Could) you (please) give me change for a dollar?
5. Would (OR Could) you (please) take a picture of me and my friends?
6. Would (OR Could) you (please) take me to the airport?
7. Would (OR Could) you (please) help me with my suitcases?
8. Would (OR Could) you (please) show me the brown shoes in the window?
9. Would (OR Could) you (please) sit down?

PART **COMPARISONS; THE PAST PROGRESSIVE**

UNIT **COMPARATIVE FORM OF ADJECTIVES**

1

✓ — 2, 3, 5, 7

2

One Syllable — fast, high, hot, long, old, small
Two Syllables — crowded, easy, friendly, heavy, messy, noisy, pretty
Three or Four Syllables — dangerous, difficult, expensive, intelligent

3

2. better
3. farther
4. more intelligent
5. worse
6. messier
7. more comfortable
8. more careful
9. prettier
10. more difficult
11. easier

4

2. longer than
3. more expensive than

4. bigger than
5. higher than
6. hotter than
7. more dangerous than
8. more crowded than
9. noisier than
10. heavier than
11. faster than
12. friendlier than

5

2. Is this unit easier or more difficult than the last unit? It is more difficult. (OR It is easier.)
3. Is this watch cheaper or more expensive than that watch? It is cheaper.
4. Are you younger or older than your best friend? I am younger (OR I am older.)
5. Are you taller or shorter than your teacher? I am taller. (OR I am shorter.)
6. Is your hometown bigger or smaller than Los Angeles? It is smaller. (OR It is bigger.)
7. Is today's weather better or worse than yesterday's weather? It is better. (OR It is worse.)

UNIT 39 ADVERBS OF MANNER AND COMPARATIVE FORMS OF ADVERBS

1

3. adverb
4. adjective
5. adverb
6. adverb
7. adverb
8. adjective
9. adjective
10. adverb
11. adverb
12. adjective

2

```
B H A P P I L Y   F
A E A S I L Y Q   A
D A N G E R O U S L Y
L V G       I   T
Y I R   P A T I E N T L Y
  L I       E
  Y L   W E L L
    Y       Y
```

3

2. quietly
3. dangerously
4. angrily
5. happily
6. well
7. badly
8. fast
9. patiently
10. easily

4

2. beautiful, beautiful
3. fast, fast
4. tired, tired
5. well, good
6. carefully, careful
7. loud, loudly (OR loud)
8. angrily, angry
9. easy, easily

5

2. harder
3. better
4. more carefully
5. faster
6. more neatly
7. worse
8. more quickly
9. more easily
10. higher
11. more rudely

UNIT **40** ADJECTIVE + *ENOUGH* / *TOO* / *VERY*; *AS* + ADJECTIVE / ADVERB + *AS*

1

2. f
3. h
4. c
5. a
6. d
7. e
8. g

2

2. The apartment is too small for six people.
3. Shirley and Jack are too slow to run in the race.
4. The car is too expensive for us to buy.
5. The children are·too young to start school.
6. The room is too cold.

3

2. The jacket isn't big enough for me.
3. The break wasn't long enough.
4. It isn't light enough to take a picture.
5. It isn't quiet enough to talk.
6. Buses aren't fast enough.

4

2. too
3. too
4. very
5. very
6. too
7. very
8. very
9. too

5

2. This coffee is too strong to drink.
3. The instructions were too difficult to understand.
4. The fruit is not ripe enough to eat.
5. The line is too long to wait.
6. The sweater was too dirty to wash by hand.
7. He is not rich enough to marry.
8. The eggs are cooked enough to eat.

6

3. too frightened
4. not big enough
5. too late
6. hot enough
7. too tight
8. too short
9. not safe enough
10. warm enough
11. not sunny enough

7

✓ — 2, 3, 4, 6, 7

8

3. as
4. than
5. as
6. than
7. as
8. as
9. as
10. than
11. than
12. than

9

4. Trains aren't as fast as airplanes.
5. January is as cold as February.
6. The chair is as comfortable as the sofa.
7. The governor of Oregon isn't as famous as the president of the United States.
8. The bank isn't as far as the post office.
9. Limes are as sour as lemons.
10. Jazz is more relaxing than rock music.
11. Chocolate ice cream isn't as good as vanilla ice cream.
12. Some people are more violent than other people.
13. College isn't as easy as high school.
14. These boxes are as heavy as those boxes.

10

2. Are you the same height as your brother?
3. Is your mother the same age as your father?
4. Is the dining room the same size as the living room?
5. Are the apples the same price as the oranges?
6. Are you the same weight as your brother?
7. Is *War and Peace* the same length as *Crime and Punishment*?
8. Is the subway station the same distance as the bus stop?

11

3. A bike is the same as a bicycle.
4. A TV is the same as a television.
5. North America is different from the United States.
6. 10,362 is different from 10.362.
7. 3 × 16 is the same as 16 × 3.
8. 16 ÷ 3 is different from 3 ÷ 16.
9. $1 is different from £1.
10. A snack bar is different from a restaurant.
11. 12:00 P.M. is the same as noon.
12. A plane is the same as an airplane.

UNIT THE PAST PROGRESSIVE

❶

(Answers will vary.)

❷

2. She was talking on the phone.
3. They were waiting for a table.
4. They were studying.
5. She was typing.
6. He was buying some groceries.
7. She was taking a shower.
8. She was cooking dinner.
9. He was getting gas.
10. He was going to school.

❸

3. wasn't reading
4. were waiting
5. weren't standing
6. was wearing

7. wasn't holding
8. wasn't buying
9. weren't leaving

❹

2. While my father was talking to me, someone rang the doorbell.
3. The boys were playing basketball when the fight started.
4. I was swimming when I got a pain in my leg.
5. When we saw the accident, we were driving down Market Street.
6. The doctor was examining Mrs. May when she screamed.
7. While I was washing my hair, I got some soap in my eyes.
8. Alan was shaving when he cut himself.
9. The train came while we were getting our tickets.

❺

2. Was he meeting with his salespeople
3. Was she teaching
4. Was he swimming
5. Was she practicing the piano
6. Was he listening to a business report on the radio
7. Were they having dinner
8. Were they watching the news
9. Was she taking a bath

❻

1b. hurried
2a. was watching
2b. answered
3a. were sleeping

3b. ran
4a. were standing
4b. sat
5a. was climbing

5b. called
6b. put

6a. was ironing

❼

2. What were you doing? (OR Why were you standing there?)
3. What were you waiting for?
4. Where were you going?
5. Why were you going to the gym?
6. Who was driving?
7. How fast was he going (OR driving)?
8. Why was he driving (OR going) so fast?
9. Who was riding?

PART MODALS II; THE SUPERLATIVE

UNIT SHOULD, SHOULDN'T, OUGHT TO, HAD BETTER, AND HAD BETTER NOT

❶

2. shouldn't
3. should
4. shouldn't
5. shouldn't
6. should

7. should
8. shouldn't
9. should
10. shouldn't

❷

2. I ought to visit my grandparents more often.
3. All passengers ought to arrive at the airport an hour before their flight.
4. Carol ought to study harder.
5. We ought to take something to the party.

❸

2. You should cook the meat a little longer.
3. Lulu should be nicer to Elenore.
4. I should learn how to type.
5. Pete and Elenore should move into a smaller apartment.

❹

2. should look for another one
3. shouldn't smoke
4. should go to the dentist
5. should wash it
6. shouldn't leave a tip
7. should study more
8. should leave early
9. shouldn't watch it
10. shouldn't touch it

5

2. Why should we have
3. How many (people) should we invite?
4. Who should we invite?
5. What should we buy?
6. What should we cook?
7. Where should we get
8. What should we do?
9. When should we send

6

a. 2, 5
b. 7, 10
c. 6
d. 4, 9
e. 3, 8

7

2. had better not serve shrimp
3. had better get a couple of bottles
4. had better not let the dog in the house
5. had better ask Costas to bring her
6. had better not sit together at the table
7. had better invite him
8. had better rent a video
9. had better borrow some from the neighbors

UNIT 43 HAVE TO, DON'T HAVE TO, MUST, MUSTN'T

1

(Answers will vary.)

2

2. have to, don't have to
3. don't have to, have to
4. have to, don't have to
5. don't have to, have to
6. have to, don't have to
7. don't have to, have to
8. have to, don't have to
9. have to, don't have to
10. don't have to, have to

3

2. has to leave early today.
3. have to go food shopping today.
4. have to come by taxi.
5. doesn't have to work late today.
6. don't have to clean up their room.
7. has to take some medicine.
8. don't have to pay for the tickets.
9. has to wear a suit and tie this morning.
10. doesn't have to do housework.

4

2. don't have to do the last exercise again.
3. didn't have to go to school yesterday.
4. had to clean her room yesterday.
5. doesn't have to write her parents every week.
6. didn't have to go shopping last week.
7. have to take tests.
8. don't have to buy a new car.
9. has to see her doctor today.
10. have to check my answers to this exercise.

5

2. You must stop.
3. You mustn't turn right.
4. You mustn't turn left.
5. You mustn't drive faster than 55 mph.
6. You mustn't park in this area.
7. You mustn't make a U-turn.
8. You mustn't pass.
9. You must go more slowly.

6

2. They had to find someone to take care of their dog.
3. They had to get to the airport on time.
4. They didn't have to get up early every morning.
5. They didn't have to go to work.
6. They had to look for a hotel.
7. They didn't have to make the bed every morning.
8. They had to pack and unpack suitcases.
9. They had to pay their hotel bill.
10. They didn't have to wash dishes.

7

2. Does your mother have to get up at 6:00 in the morning? Yes, she does. (OR No, she doesn't.)
3. Did you have to cook last night? Yes, I did. (OR No, I didn't.)
4. Does your best friend have to do this exercise? Yes, he / she does. (OR No, he / she doesn't.)
5. Do you have to be in English class on time? Yes, I do. (OR No, I don't.)
6. Do your friends have to learn English? Yes, they do. (OR No, they don't.)
7. Did your father have to shave yesterday? Yes, he did. (OR No, he didn't.)
8. Did your best friend have to go to work yesterday? Yes, he / she did. (OR No, he / she didn't.)
9. Did you have to take a test last week? Yes, I did. (OR No, I didn't.)

8

2. does she have to get a book from the library?
3. does he have to go?
4. did the teacher have to talk to?
5. did you have to stay there?
6. do the students have to stay after class?
7. do you have to use?
8. did the high school students have to send their college applications?
9. do you have to get up?
10. did he have to borrow?

UNIT 44 SUPERLATIVE FORM OF ADJECTIVES AND ADVERBS

1

2. Doug
3. Norma
4. Carol
5. Norma
6. Carol

2

2. the worst
3. the hardest
4. the most beautiful
5. the busiest
6. the funniest
7. the best
8. the ugliest
9. the most popular
10. the lowest
11. the fastest
12. the most charming

3

(Answers for part b of each question will vary.)
2a. A teenager is the oldest of the three.
2b. A child is older than a baby.
3a. A Rolls Royce is the most expensive of the three.
3b. A BMW is more expensive than a Ford.
4a. Nigeria is the hottest of the three.
4b. Spain is hotter than Sweden.
5a. A highway is the widest of the three.
5b. A street is wider than a path.
6a. A city is the biggest of the three.
6b. A town is bigger than a village.
7a. An elephant is the heaviest of the three.
7b. A gorilla is heavier than a fox.
8a. An hour is the longest of the three.
8b. A minute is longer than a second.
9a. Boxing is the most dangerous of the three.
9b. Soccer is more dangerous than golf.
10a. Chocolate is the most fattening of the three.
10b. A banana is more fattening than a carrot.

4

1b. Andy came the earliest.
2a. The red car is going the most slowly (OR the slowest).

2b. The white car is going the fastest.
3a. Fran drives the most dangerously.
3b. Shirley drives the most carefully.
4a. Gary works the closest to his home.
4b. Harris works the farthest from his home.
5a. Carolyn speaks Spanish the best.
5b. Milton speaks Spanish the worst.
6a. Renée types the most quickly (OR the quickest).
6b. Joan types the most accurately.

PUTTING IT ALL TOGETHER

REVIEW OF VERB TENSES AND MODALS

1

2. We <u>are having</u> a wonderful time on our honeymoon.
3. Venice <u>is</u> such a romantic place
4. It <u>has</u> so many beautiful places.
5. Yesterday, we <u>walked</u> all around the city.
6. We <u>visited</u> several churches.
7. They <u>were</u> so wonderful
8. we <u>saw</u> so many gorgeous paintings
9. we <u>didn't go</u> far from our hotel
10. This afternoon, we <u>had</u> lunch
11. We both <u>ate</u> special Venetian dishes
12. Dan <u>is</u> resting
13. we <u>are going to</u> take a gondola ride

2

2. Where is their hotel?
3. What are they going to do tonight?
4. Why did they stay in their hotel last night?
5. Where are they going today?
6. What time will the tour start?
7. What is Dan doing?
8. Who is the tour guide?
9. Where are they going to have dinner (in the evening)?
10. Who are they going to have dinner with?
11. When did Carol and Dan meet two people from Canada?
12. What are the two people's names?
13. How long are Paul and Myra going to stay in Venice?
14. Who does Carol like a lot?
15. Why was Dan sick all night?
16. What does Dan love to do?

3

2. a	5. b	8. b	11. a
3. a	6. b	9. a	
4. a	7. b	10. b	

REVIEW OF VERB TENSES AND COMPARISONS

2. Teacher A is more organized than Teacher B.
3. Teacher A is nicer than Teacher B.
4. Teacher A teaches better than Teacher B.
5. Teacher A speaks more clearly than Teacher B.
6. Teacher A is friendlier than Teacher B.
7. Teacher A gives back homework more quickly than Teacher B.
8. Teacher A explains things more slowly than Teacher B.
9. The atmosphere in Teacher A's class is more relaxed than the atmosphere in Teacher B's class.
10. The homework in Teacher A's class is easier than the homework in Teacher B's class.
11. The books in Teacher A's class are more interesting than the books in Teacher B's class.
12. Unfortunately, the tests in Teacher A's class are harder than the tests in Teacher B's class.

2

2. Teacher B isn't as organized as Teacher A.
3. Teacher B isn't as nice as Teacher A.
4. Teacher B doesn't teach as well as Teacher A.
5. Teacher B doesn't speak as clearly as Teacher A.
6. Teacher B isn't as friendly as Teacher A.
7. Teacher B doesn't give back homework as quickly as Teacher A.
8. Teacher B doesn't explain things as slowly as Teacher A.
9. The atmosphere in Teacher B's class isn't as relaxed as the atmosphere in Teacher A's class.
10. The homework in Teacher B's class isn't as easy as the homework in Teacher A's class.
11. The books in Teacher B's class aren't as interesting as the books in Teacher A's class.
12. The tests in Teacher B's class aren't as hard as the tests in Teacher A's class.

REVIEW OF VERB TENSES, NOUNS, AND QUANTIFIERS

2. There are a few glasses in the first picture, but there are a lot of glasses in the second picture.
3. There are a lot of flowers in the first picture, but there are a few flowers in the second picture.
4. There is a lot of Coke in the first picture, but there is a little Coke in the second picture.
5. There is a little chocolate in the first picture, but there is a lot of chocolate in the second picture.
6. There are a few candles on the cake in the first picture, but there are a lot of candles on the cake in the second picture.
7. There is a lot of fruit in the first picture, but there is a little fruit in the second picture.
8. There is a lot of cheese in the first picture, but there is a little cheese in the second picture.
9. There is a little bread in the first picture, but there is a lot of bread in the second picture.
10. There are a few gifts in the first picture, but there are a lot of gifts in the second picture.

2

2. Is there much bread? No, there isn't.
3. Is there much butter? No, there isn't.
4. Are there many chairs? Yes, there are.
5. Is there much cheese? Yes, there is.
6. Is there much chocolate? No, there isn't.
7. Are there many flowers? Yes, there are.
8. Is there much fruit? Yes, there is.
9. Are there many gifts? No, there aren't.
10. Are there many glasses? No, there aren't.
11. Is there much orange juice? Yes, there is.
12. Are there many potato chips? Yes, there are.